A YEAR IN THE LIFE: Journaling for Self-Discovery

to the white,
imagination
e explorer to
he leap and
looked at

writer,
Writers

and accessi-
rmat, Sheila
geable
agmented
from a vari-
urge us to

erapist

race *A Year*
one and
worth of
a welcome

—*Kathleen Adams, M.A., L.P.C.*

author of The Journal to the Self *and* The Write Way
to Wellness, *director of The Center for Journal Therapy*

A YEAR in the L🌷FE

JOURNALING FOR SELF-DISCOVERY

SHEILA BENDER

WALKING STICK PRESS
CINCINNATI, OHIO
www.writersdigest.com

Visit our Web site at www.writersdigest.com for information on more resources for writers.

To receive a free weekly E-mail newsletter delivering tips and updates about writing and about Writer's Digest products, send an E-mail with "Subscribe Newsletter" in the body of the message to newsletter-request@writersdigest .com, or register directly at our Web site at www.writersdigest.com.

04′ 03 02 01 00   5 4 3 2 1

Library of Congress Cataloging-in-Publication Data

Bender, Sheila
   A year in the life: journaling for self-discovery / by Sheila Bender.—1st ed.
     p.   cm.
   Includes index.
   ISBN 0-89879-971-6 (pbk.)
     1. Diaries—Authorship. 2. Diaries—Authorship—Psychological aspects. I. Title.

PN4390.B46   2000
808′.02—dc21   00-022817
                                                         CIP

Editors: Jack Heffron and Meg Leder
Designer: Sandy Conopeotis Kent
Cover designed by: Cindy Beckmeyer/Beckmeyer Design
Cover illustration by: Lisa Ballard
Author photo by: Pranesh Cadman
Production coordinator: Emily Gross

FOR *Virginia Mann*
HOME BASE WINTER, 1999

ACKNOWLEDGMENTS

I want to thank my editor at Writer's Digest Books, Jack Heffron, and the people at the press for trusting my voice and for making room for this book in their new Writer's Spirit Series. I also want to thank the students who worked with my exercises and allowed me to publish their journal entries. A special thanks to all of those in Tucson, Arizona, and Port Townsend, Washington, who helped me spend a healthy, comfortable winter away working on this book: Kurt VanderSluis, Virginia and Larry Mann, Diana Madaras, Susan Prust, Barbara Adler, John Nemorovski, Marlee Millman, Sally Showalter, Lauren Smith, Susan Scholl, Marcie Bowman, Helen Murdoch, Susan Dick, Judy and Jim Tough, and Kathryn DeLong. Special appreciation goes to Julia Rouse for her help in discovering journal keeping resources and to Nancy Linnon for sharing her library and her office with me.

 Sheila Bender has been writing and teaching writing since 1981. Her poems and essays appear in many North American literary magazines. She writes a monthly poetry column for *Writer's Digest* magazine and is on the faculty of the summer Colorado Mountain Writer's Conference in Glenwood Springs, Colorado. She teaches writing, including keeping a writer's journal, for the University of Arizona's Extended University, as well as for continuing education and university programs in Los Angeles. To find out more, visit her Web site at www .SheilaBender.com.

TABLE OF CONTENTS

CHAPTER ONE

Defining the Writer's Journal | *1*

A Definition of the Journiary | *3*

From Evocation We Gain Insight | *4*

CHAPTER TWO

What Psychologists, Scholars and Writers Say About Keeping a Journal | *7*

Journaling Aids in Total Life Development | *7*

Journaling Helps You De-Stress | *9*

Journaling Enhances Creative Thinking | *10*

Journaling Helps You Write Well | *12*

Journaling Increases Feelings of Connection to Self and Community | *13*

CHAPTER THREE

Putting Together a Journal That Works for You | *15*

What Does Your Journal Look Like? | *16*

Putting the Journal Together | *22*

What Your Journal Is Made Of | *24*

Adding in Extras | *25*

Exploring Issues of Privacy | *29*

Exploring Issues of Commitment | *30*

CHAPTER FOUR

Hiring the Journal Keeper Within | 35

Creating a Job Description That Works | 37

Interviewing the Candidate | 41

Designate a Start Date and Place of Employment | 42

How to Proceed Using The Next Chapters | 42

Troubleshooting | 43

CHAPTER FIVE

First Quarter | 47

WEEK ONE: Dialogues to Diffuse the Power of Critical Voices | 48

WEEK TWO: A Lesson From Morrie and Rilke | 52

WEEK THREE: Letter to a Columnist | 56

WEEK FOUR: Reading, Writing and 'Rithmatic, Taught to the Tune of What I Did | 58

WEEK FIVE: Cider Mills and Burning Leaves | 61

WEEK SIX: The Interruption That Became an Inspiration | 64

WEEK SEVEN: Grandma's Closet | 66

WEEK EIGHT: Finding the Tourist Within | 67

WEEK NINE: Finding the Motto Writer Within | 69

WEEK TEN: Metaphor for My Life Right Now | 71

WEEK ELEVEN: The Words They Taught Me | 73

WEEK TWELVE: Return to Morrie's Window | 74

WEEK THIRTEEN: Self-Reflection Week | 76

CHAPTER SIX

Second Quarter | *81*

WEEK FOURTEEN: A Walker in the City, Town or Village | *81*

WEEK FIFTEEN: Soul Between the Lines | *83*

WEEK SIXTEEN: Affirm, Affirm, Affirm | *84*

WEEK SEVENTEEN: Confetti | *85*

WEEK EIGHTEEN: Chasing the Caribou | *87*

WEEK NINETEEN: Before and After | *88*

WEEK TWENTY: I Know How to Do This | *90*

WEEK TWENTY-ONE: There Ought to Be a Word for This | *92*

WEEK TWENTY-TWO: If I Were a Rich Man | *93*

WEEK TWENTY-THREE: This Is a Story About | *94*

WEEK TWENTY-FOUR: Things to Do | *96*

WEEK TWENTY-FIVE: Burying the Dutch Oven | *98*

WEEK TWENTY-SIX: Self-Reflection Week | *99*

CHAPTER SEVEN

Third Quarter | *103*

WEEK TWENTY-SEVEN: Owning a Place | *104*

WEEK TWENTY-EIGHT: Each Side a Balance | *105*

WEEK TWENTY-NINE: Recipes | *108*

WEEK THIRTY: Private Moments | *109*

WEEK THIRTY-ONE: Your Perfect Opposite | *110*

WEEK THIRTY-TWO: Gratitude | *112*

WEEK THIRTY-THREE: Shopping | *114*

WEEK THIRTY-FOUR: Eating With Others | *116*

WEEK THIRTY-FIVE: To Thine Own Self Be True | *118*

WEEK THIRTY-SIX: Admonitions | *119*

WEEK THIRTY-SEVEN: Six of One, Half a Dozen of the Other | *121*

WEEK THIRTY-EIGHT: What It Takes | *123*
WEEK THIRTY-NINE: Self-Reflection Week | *124*

CHAPTER EIGHT

Fourth Quarter | *127*

WEEK FORTY: First You Have to Teach a Lesson | *127*
WEEK FORTY-ONE: Self-Portrait, Self-Portrait on the Wall | *130*
WEEK FORTY-TWO: Bridges of Your County | *131*
WEEK FORTY-THREE: Sacredness in Everyday Life | *133*
WEEK FORTY-FOUR: Hide-and-Seek | *135*
WEEK FORTY-FIVE: Whistling | *137*
WEEK FORTY-SIX: Starvation Hill | *138*
WEEK FORTY-SEVEN: Getting Here | *140*
WEEK FORTY-EIGHT: Bureks | *142*
WEEK FORTY-NINE: Here Lies My Heart | *144*
WEEK FIFTY: Scenes | *145*
WEEK FIFTY-ONE: Penultimate | *148*
WEEK FIFTY-TWO: Self-Reflection Week | *150*

CHAPTER NINE

Journal Writing for Life Occasions and Holidays | *153*

Eight Life Occasions

Birthdays | *153*
Marriages | *154*
Divorces | *155*
Deaths | *156*
Births | *157*
Anniversaries | *158*
Endings and Beginnings | *158*

Holidays and Other Observances

New Year's Day | *160*
Ramadan | *162*
Martin Luther King Day | *163*
Valentine's Day | *163*
St. Patrick's Day | *164*
Passover | *164*
April Fools' Day | *165*
Easter | *165*
Cinco de Mayo | *166*
Mother's Day | *166*
Memorial Day | *167*
Father's Day | *167*
Indpendence Day | *168*
Labor Day | *169*
Rosh Hashanah and Yom Kippur | *169*
Halloween | *170*
Thanksgiving | *171*
Hanukkah | *172*
Christmas | *173*
Kwanzaa | *173*

CHAPTER TEN

Resources to Help Journal Keepers Continue Writing | *175*

Books on Journal Keeping | *175*

Centers for Help With Journal Keeping | *182*

Newsletters and Magazines About Journal Keeping | *184*

APPENDIX

Mini-Anthology of Sample Journal Entries
From the Exercises | *187*

CONTRIBUTORS' NOTES | *215*

INDEX | *218*

... it is possible to return to myself, to return to this flow,
at any time, anywhere, even for just a short time span.

—BURGHILD NINA HOLZER
A Walk Between Heaven and Earth:
A Personal Journal on Writing and the Creative Process

Defining the Writer's Journal

> . . . diaries shall forever whisper from their
> cupboards . . . *I was, I was—I am.*
>
> THOMAS MALLON
> *"Epilogue," A Book of One's Own: People and Their Diaries*

These days most people know something about keeping a journal. Teachers, therapists, support group leaders and others in the helping professions have been advocating journal keeping for years. Memoirists, family history writers and genealogy buffs talk about using the journals of ancestors and relatives. Oprah Winfrey talks to her television audience about journaling. Bookstores and gift stores stock shelves with decoratively covered blank books, some with inspirational quotations and prompts for starting writing.

Most of us now call writing personal material on a regular basis journaling, but if you are a woman, you may remember being ten or eleven, and starting to write in a white or pink leatherette-covered five-year diary with a fragile lock and a key so small it always got lost. If you are a man, you may remember peeking into such a diary when no one was looking and then teasing your sister to tears. All of you may have memories of explorers' logs read in school, and you may wonder if there are differences between keeping a diary or keeping a journal and if such differences matter.

Some theorists believe the term "diary" has a feminine connotation and the term "journal" a masculine connotation, which, they say, lends more importance to the journal. In this thinking, diaries are about daily, mundane matters, while journals, kept more sporadically but with longer entries, weigh in on the heavier side of exploring life issues and questions. Christina Baldwin, well-known author of books on journaling, says in *Life's Companion: Journal Writing as a Spiritual Quest*, that the diary is more formal with its daily entries and is outwardly focused on the writer's activities, experiences and observations while the journal is "an intermittent record of the inner life, written consistently, but not necessarily on a daily basis." Fiction writer Robin Hemley, writing in *The Writer's Journal: 40 Contemporary Writers and Their Journals*, believes "diarists seem, as a whole, fascinated with their own lives—journal-keepers are snoops, fascinated with everyone else's life." William G. Hartley wrote that "because the designation 'journalist' normally applies to professional writers, we favor calling anyone who writes a diary or a personal journal a 'diarist.'" Curtis W. Casewit titled his 1982 book on the subject, *The Diary: A Complete Guide to Journal Writing*. The interchangeable quality of the terms has led other writers such as Denise Levertov, Robert Hellenga and Omar S. Castaneda to use the word "notebooks."

The word "journal" has in its root the word *jour*, French for day. A journey was the distance that could be traveled in a day. A journal, therefore, consisted of the writing one recorded per day. The word "diary" comes from the Latin *diarium*, meaning daily food or allowance. What person wanting to write hasn't thought of how much time they can allow themselves to write, to contemplate, to create the thoughts and observations that nurture them? Keeping a diary or a journal is a way to make sure there is time to create that food. Perhaps we should call the kind of book I am about to encourage you to keep a "journiary," or better yet, since this one is to cover a year's time, maybe it should be called an "annualiary."

Whatever you call it (and even a name like Betsy or Art could do well, since it is a friend you'll be "conversing" with), as you make entries from the prompts and writing ideas in this book, you will borrow from the techniques writers, travelers, adventurers, psychologists and spiritual leaders use in their personal writing. By offering prompts, writing occasions, strategies and exercises, I hope to help you write freely about the fact that you are writing to know more of yourself. By offering self-reflection exercises to be done four times a year, I hope to help you look into your own creative efforts and recognize the voice within, the one that talks about the world your way and speaks ever more interestingly about both it and yourself.

According to Agnes De Mille, "Living is a form of not being sure, not knowing what's next or how. The moment you know how, you begin to die a little. The artist never entirely knows. We guess. We may be wrong, but we take leap after leap in the dark." My prompts and self-reflection questions are meant to help you journey in your pages as an artist journeys in life.

A Definition of the Journiary

Your blank book, loose-leaf papers or computer are where you can make sure that by thinking in writing, you allow yourself to take leaps in the dark. In such places, you can write every day or week in a quest to keep describing your world from a state in which you are present in the moment but not knowing what is next. If you write from this state, you will find writing offers you epiphanies, meaningful evocations of places and people and things past and present, as well as knowledge essential to your well-being that you would not have been able to gain any other way.

Writing is wiser than we are, many writers say. As a poet and essayist this has been my experience. I let the writing lead me, and the whole time it is leading me, I must be careful to remain unknowing. I must not set my will upon the words. I must let them flow as they wish to. My job is to keep them coming through my center, not my head, and only in that way will the writing steer wisdom's course. I will teach you how to make journal entries in which you write about what you see or remember with an attitude or stance of not knowing, so that new wisdom and experience will arrive.

From Evocation We Gain Insight

Through the years, society's observers, writers, artists and travelers have kept journals in order to think in writing about cultures and creativity. Now that self-help professionals advocate journaling as a tool for self-discovery, the emphasis is on finding oneself. Recent discussions of journaling, though, too often ignore how the *craft* of writing itself is a powerful tool for the careful observation that leads to insight. We can do much more in our journals besides writing with phrases like "finding my creative side," "getting my anger out" and "freeing myself up." We can evoke the texture and complexities of this world and from evocation gain insight. We are privileged today to have so much to read in nonfiction, fiction and poetry. These works suggest ways to journal that will aid in mining the unconscious for ideas and insight rather than mere repetitive cathartic phrases and circular introspection.

Today, we need to do more than find our voices in anger, sadness and joy. We also need to find ourselves mirrored in the natural world and in our families, work and cultural surroundings. We need to write of the outside to more thoroughly see the inside. We must accept that what we have created and live with on the outside is sometimes a manifestation of the chaos, blindness and crushing attitudes we let prevail on the inside. We must also see how the mystery, peace and lyric quality of life exists in our outer and our inner world. "Wholeness has become necessary," Anne Hazard Aldrich writes in *Notes From Myself: A Guide to Creative Journal Writing*:

> We each have the potential to be our own Virgil by sitting down and writing about our life. Amazing paths appear when our subconscious is released in writing. . . . Writing is clarifying; it is not an impenetrable mystery to be avoided. Its mysteries are those of enlightenment. Exploring the mystery of ourselves is a lifesaving act of bravery; it is saying, "Yes, I will make discoveries, and I will take journeys offered. I will know myself."

How can one take this journey when the only map is in the actual journey? How can one draw this map when the journey itself is only beginning? How can one map a journey upon which one is always wondering which way to turn, as well as whether to continue at all? I believe making entries using techniques that force us to observe our surroundings, the people and our interactions yields a method by which to draw this map and take the journey.

It was the English poet William Blake who wrote, "To See a World in a Grain of Sand." When I read the poem's title, I know that though the grain of sand is inanimate, when we touch it and hear the water around it, taste the salt on it and feel the crack of it against our teeth, we come to know ourselves. The more we know of ourselves, the more we are of this world.

Jungian analyst Marion Woodman has written:

> Soulmaking is allowing the eternal essence to enter and experience the outer world through all the orifices of the body—seeing, smelling, hearing, tasting, touching—so that the soul grows during its time on Earth. . . . Soulmaking is constantly

confronting the paradox that an eternal being is dwelling in a temporal body.

We can use writing to allow the "eternal essence to enter and experience the outer world" through our senses. Then, we become more alive. It may sometimes seem difficult and a chore to do this writing. Something in us just doesn't want to budge from a state of slumber and disconnection. But by using our senses, our beings are refreshed and brought more fully alive. Writing using our senses helps us feel how alive we are because we re-create our experiences as they were lived—through the five senses.

My hope is that by doing the exercises in this book, journaling will become something that keeps you going, peps you up and becomes as necessary and as health-providing as exercise. I hope you will crave doing it and become ever more yourself and ever more in love with the world, its peaks and valleys, its rough spots and smooth waters, its sunny days and stormy ones, its droughts and floods.

∞

Before we get to the specific techniques that will help you journal, let's look at what experts have said about the ways journaling can help you emotionally, spiritually, physically, as well as with your writing.

CHAPTER TWO

What Psychologists, Scholars and Writers Say About Keeping a Journal

On these clear, empty pages, parts of me have been born and nurtured into maturity.

MARION WOODMAN
Jungian analyst, in her Foreword to Marlene A. Schiwy's
A Voice of Her Own: Women and the Journal-Writing Journey

I know from friends who keep journals, my own endeavors and those of students in my journal writing classes, how much writing each day or once a week means, whether the writing is done playfully, in serious moods or during times of boredom that invariably alter themselves during the act of writing. I have developed a deeper understanding about the value of journal keeping from listening to the words of those who have made a life's work out of studying the connection between journal keeping and self-development, spirituality and mental health.

Journaling Aids in Total Life Development

Psychotherapist Ira Progoff, founder of the Intensive Journal Workshop, notes in his book that in his practice, a personal journal and a specific process he calls Journal Feedback "establishes a person's sense of his own being by enriching his inner life with new experiences of a creative and spiritual quality." He writes, too, that journaling allows a "recognition of the inner movement and meaning of our lives," and in this light, "it actually seems that we can now begin our life anew."

University of Texas at Austin psychology professor James W. Pennebaker has written a chapter in his book *Opening Up: The Healing Power of Confiding in Others* titled "Understanding the Value of Writing." Writing about trauma, he says, helps people heal. "People reach an understanding of the events and, once this is accomplished, they no longer need to inhibit their talking any further." It is the inhibiting of the talk that causes problems.

In *Making Sense of Suffering*, J. Konrad Stettbacher, German therapist and colleague of famed psychoanalyst Alice Miller, writes (italics are his): *"There is no healing alternative to recognizing and facing the truth."* And he continues:

> We must help ourselves to examine and re-examine our own behavior and that of others, then do it again to achieve an ever-clearer picture of the confused situation we are in. . . . As adults we are the sole judge presiding over our lives and taking responsibility for the future.

Stettbacher says the kind of therapy required for this growth can be done with writing. In the first step, which he names Perception (present or recalled), the writer names what he or she is sensing, noticing, seeing, hearing and smelling.

Paul and Patricia D'Encarnacao, husband and wife psychologist and medical doctor team, wrote in their book *The Joy of Journaling:*

> If we could only begin to see patterns to our lives. If we could only get some correct answers or even ask the right question.

If we could only see what may be coming down the road for us. If only we could alleviate some of the stress and pressure of everyday life. All these ifs can become yeses if we begin to work with ourselves and journal in earnest.

Journaling Helps You De-Stress

Paul Pearsall, Ph.D., clinical and educational psychologist, explains in *Write Your Own Pleasure Prescription: 60 Ways to Create Balance and Joy in Your Life*, that you can write anger away instead of letting it blow up into aggression.

Underneath anger and frustration are other feelings. Writing exercises can help you get to them. John Gardner advised in his book *The Art of Fiction: Notes on Craft for Young Writers* that students write two pieces about the same lake, one a description of the lake from the point of view of a man who has just fallen in love, and the other a description of the same lake from the point of view of a man who has just committed a murder. The writer was not to state the love or the murder. When angry, you could write describing something without revealing the target of your anger and profit from the evocation whether you are describing a lake or a meal set before you. Then switch gears and write a description of the same place or thing from the point of view of feeling happy because something good has happened, like getting a raise, recognition or an invitation. You'll learn to let all kinds of feelings out and experience balance.

Another psychologist, Dr. Daniel Mroczek of Fordham University, found in a study that age correlates with happiness because older people are able to make happier choices than younger people—they actively take steps to bring beneficial experiences into their lives and minimize experiences that wear on their spirits. Certainly, just as we can write anger away, we can learn to use a journal to increase the beneficial experiences we are having! Creative writing allows us to meld with our environment and see our inner ideals and transactions. Many people report a sense of serenity after journaling, even if they have been writing about unhappy times or conflicts. Perhaps this is a phenomenon related to what Jesus says in one of the Gnostic Gospels: "If you bring forth what is within you, what you bring forth will save you. If you do not bring forth what is in you, what you do not bring forth will destroy you."

Journaling Enhances Creative Thinking

Actor, musician, TV program creator and author Steve Allen was interviewed by *Bottom Line/Personal* magazine, February 1, 1999, on mind improvement. He said too often people fall in love with their first answer, but jumping to conclusions stifles creativity. According to Allen, "I don't know" is one of the wisest things you can say. "By remaining open to many possibilities, you get out of your own way so that you can think more creatively." Certainly a journal is the right place to practice thinking from the I-don't-know-place.

In *The Writer's Journal: 40 Contemporary Writers and Their Journals*, poet Brenda Hillman wrote that keeping a journal is "the assurance of a sacred space. . . . There is only the purity of unstudied thought." In the same anthology, poet William Matthews wrote, "And 'idea' is too big a word. It's not scrappy enough. An idea might lead to another, and thence to the exposition of an argument and from there to the discovery of an intellectual pattern. . . ." Better, he thought, to keep a journal "the way a cook might tend a good strain of yeast or mother-of-vinegar." Novelist Lisa Shea contributed this:

> My journal-writing has served primarily as a repository of secrets and experiences, a place where observations and opin-

ions, feelings and facts intersect and entwine. I have used the journal to record daydreams and nightmares, wishes, fantasies, cruelties and conundrums, to relax and to scrutinize. It is where I tell the truth, and the place where I fashion lies.

Leadership consultant Michael J. Gelb underlines the importance of not knowing in his book, *How to Think Like Leonardo da Vinci: Seven Steps to Genius Every Day*. He suggests keeping a journal to record observations, ideas and questions as Leonardo did. He says not to focus on goals or results, but to let thoughts flow and see where they lead. The journal is the place not to have answers so much as to have the opportunity to explore. He suggests writing three of your beliefs in your journal, then making a case for the opposite belief to examine your views from multiple perspectives.

G. Lynn Nelson, professor of English at Arizona State University and director of the Greater Phoenix Area Writing Project, says we must undo some of what we have been taught about language and use language in our journals as it was once used—to evoke mystery. In *Writing and Being: Taking Back Our Lives Through the Power of Language*, Nelson says, "Too often in school, we study language and writing in isolation, apart from the people who speak and write and apart from what happens when people speak and write." He says teachers "play sad little games with language—circling misspelled words and dangling participles, making students feel small and stupid, and turning them away from the power of their own words."

Nelson, in his fervor, wants to grab all those who think language is only the study of adjectives and pronouns and grammatical constructions and say:

. . . no one knows why between the ages of one and four, language emerges from within each of us, why we become incredibly, amazingly proficient at language, without ever cracking a grammar book or taking a test or even meeting an English teacher. But it happens. The gift of language emerges within us and waits there for us to find its power.

We get more instruction in this way of viewing language and writing from the German poet Rainer Maria Rilke, famous in America for the letters he wrote to a young poet querying him about whether his poetry had merit in the eyes of the master. Rilke says:

> . . . describe your sorrows and desires, passing thoughts and the belief in some sort of beauty—describe all these with loving, quiet, humble sincerity, and use, to express yourself, the things in your environment, the images from your dreams, and the objects of your memory. If your daily life seems poor, do not blame it; blame yourself, tell yourself that you are not poet enough to call forth its riches; for to the creator there is no poverty and no poor indifferent place.

Describe, Rilke says, not judge, generalize or extrapolate. Describe even the places you think are bereft of images. This way of writing peels off the layers of learning that tell us we must know what we are writing about. This is a way to come to your journaling in a state of not-knowing to find again and again the deep power language bestows.

Journaling Helps You Write Well

And if you need to know journaling is a practical use of time as well as helpful to your health and spirit, there are the words of Helen Gurley Brown, former editor in chief of *Cosmopolitan* magazine, current editor in chief of thirty-seven international editions of the magazine, and author of *The Writer's Rules: The Power of Positive Prose—How to Create It and Get It Published*. In the same issue of *Bottom Line/Personal* in which Steve Allen was interviewed, Brown said that keeping a journal helps one write well. You have to write a lot to write well, she said. She keeps a journal because it helps her express freely what's on the inside. Only after you do this, she says, can you express yourself well to others. Brown concentrates on writing about things that interest, alarm, excite or depress her. She sometimes writes an ending paragraph on what she would like to do about these things.

Journaling Increases Feelings of Connection to Self and Community

A journal is a place to feel your own being through the power of language. There is power in getting words onto a page, power in saying what you feel like saying, power in identifying what alarms, excites or depresses *you in particular*. And certainly there is power in saying, if only to yourself, what you would do or want done in a situation. But even as you take this power, remember there is no rushing perception. It is, according to Rilke, not "about reckoning and counting, but ripening like the tree. . . ." "Patience," he says, "is everything!" Yes, we must be patient with ourselves, but still we can grow our words on the page from the seeds of the exercises in this book. Then there will be something that will fruit and ripen!

It is not only ourselves personally, though, that journaling helps. Increasing our own feelings of connection can help the entire culture. Ervin Staub, University of Massachusetts at Amherst scholar, has written about the creation and evolution of caring, connection and nonaggression in his book *The Roots of Evil: The Origins of Genocide and Other Group Violence*:

Language shapes experience. Those who destroy often use euphemisms. The language of nuclear policy creates illusions: by referring to shields, umbrellas, deterrence, and "defense," it implies a security that does not exist. A language true to reality will motivate people to join in efforts to eliminate the potential of nuclear destruction.

A journal is the perfect place to learn the ways in which language communicates authenticity as opposed to the way language is a tool used by political, advertising and marketing coalitions to make us purchase something, to make us hate this group or that one, and to make us look through blurry eyes at the daily transgressions against freedom and humanity. Learning the authenticity of your own voice makes it harder and harder to write in an inauthentic voice or listen to one; it makes it harder to believe what others want you to believe against your inner will.

If you feel that taking time for journal keeping is somehow selfish and beside the point when so many "important" things are waiting to be done, just remember how important authenticity is to your well-being in a world that works against finding it and maintaining it. The more you can change yourself in the direction of your truths, the more you will make contact with and insist on the truth inside others. In this way, every journal entry is birdsong. Can you imagine a world without that?

∞

I hope you are eager to prepare a journal you will enjoy sitting down to. That is what comes next.

CHAPTER THREE

Putting Together a Journal That Works for You

Everything that holds power appears humble.

CAROLINE MYSS

What should a journal look like? In her book *One to One: Self-Understanding Through Journal Writing*, Christina Baldwin describes her bookshelf of journals as "over four feet long, an eclectic collection of differing styles, sizes, widths, formats. There are years of loose-leaf notebooks, bound in cardboard binders, and years of blank books—no longer blank, but filled with a tangible record of my life." In *A Voice of Her Own: Women and the Journal-Writing Journey*, Marlene Schiwy writes about living in London in the 1980s and discovering reasonably priced Chartwell Students Manuscript books with brightly colored linen covers. She says they fit her budget and her handbag and she not only stocked up on return visits to London, but had friends carry a few to her when they were visiting. Some people use calendars that offer one full page per day.

There are many, many idiosyncrasies involved in journal writing. Some journal keepers care about the aesthetics of the pen they use and the weight of the paper in the journal. Some journal keepers need to be sure the book opens all the way, as spiral-bound books do, so they are not fighting the binding for room to write. Some people are concerned with size because they want to carry the journal with them. They may want to sit away from a desk and comfortably write in the book, which requires a certain size for comfort in their laps and hard covers to write against. Some people want to type and paste sheets of paper into a journal or print their entries on three-hole punch paper. Many don't want the expense of a journal to be too high, yet others want to endow their ritual with significance by spending money on it.

What Does Your Journal Look Like?

My advice is: (1) Start with a regular spiral-bound notebook that you can easily purchase again. You can go on to fill many of these notebooks, and you can keep them neatly together on a shelf or in a cardboard magazine box. (2) Alternatively, write yourself a letter about what you want from your journal and see how you can get or physically put together such a journal. In fact, even if you already know you are going to go the notebook route or you already have a blank book ready to use, do this assignment. It will help you see your journal and the way you keep it as an outgrowth of who you are and what you desire.

Begin With a Cluster

Get out a piece of paper and in the center of the paper write "My Perfect Journal." Circle the phrase and as soon as you think of a characteristic that fits your idea of your journal, e.g., "fabric-covered," write the word or phrase somewhere outside that circle. Draw a line between it and the circled phrase in the middle of your page. Elaborate that characteristic with more details—e.g., "blue cotton the color of sky." Each time you write down a detail, circle it and connect that circle to the phrase that spurred you on. So from the circled "blue cotton the color of sky" might come "white speckles" and "like pinhead-sized clouds," each circled and connected to the sky image. If that reminds you of your grandmother's curtains, write that, too, and connect it to the words that inspired the association. This writing exercise is called "clustering," and it helps you gather ideas and images in a nonthreatening way. Don't worry about what you will do with these phrases; just keep imagining the characteristics of your favorite journal. Each time you feel finished jotting down bits and pieces of such a characteristic, let your mind roam to a new characteristic. Write it down, circle it and connect it to the circle in the center. Let yourself dream up details about that new characteristic. Circle and connect those. Pretty soon you have something that looks like a cluster of grapes filling the page.

You can use this technique whenever you are beginning a journal writing entry if you can't think of what to write about or if you need a relaxed way to gather the images and details of your experience.

On page 18, you'll find a sample cluster. Notice how it sprawls over the space available on the page. If you find yourself cramping words into only part of the page, you are probably also cramping your thoughts and imagination. Be strict with yourself about drawing the circles. It is the pattern-making part of ourselves that comes up with truth and original ideas. Making circles invites that part of ourselves to the page.

Dear Journal-to-Be

Begin with a fresh sheet of paper, or if you're using a computer, create a new document. Write or type the date and the salutation, "Dear Journal-to-Be." Keep your cluster beside you for reference, and begin writing or typing. Let yourself continue without stopping to think too much and without correcting errors or wording. Do this kind of writing for ten to twenty minutes. Not stopping and not correcting yourself is very important. Remember, you are inviting your very being to come forward and get involved in this new

17

Sample Cluster illustration

venture. Worrying about mistakes will only make this part of you feel hesitant and inadequate. Write with the same allowing nature you'd adopt if a young child was babbling to you or an elderly person was making you a cup of tea. You would smile and pay attention and be pleased for the effort. So set a timer or just trust yourself to keep going. Keep your pen's point to the page or your fingers on the keyboard. Every time you lift the pen from the page or your fingers from the keyboard, you create a space for your stopping, closing down, judging nature to tear your ideas apart. You don't need your ideas torn apart; you need to playfully and sincerely write them out.

Write about some of the images and details that came up in your cluster. More images will arrive as you are writing. Don't worry about how these all string together; just concentrate on writing a letter to your soon-to-be-born journal. Tell it things like where it will live and where it will visit. Tell it what you like and dislike about the physical characteristics of other people's journals and what shape, size and thickness you hope it to be. This letter tells your soon-to-be-born journal what else it might hold besides paper. I think it is only fair to mention in your letter that after it is born, the journal will be allowed to have a direction of its own and you will be willing to listen and help it grow and evolve, but for now, in order to create the journal you need, you are required to be the project leader. There are really no restrictions on how this journal shapes up. You are the creator, and your creation is just on paper for now, so don't edit any of your wildest, most far-fetched ideas, images, thoughts and associations. If you want your journal to have a voice, endow it with one. If you want your journal to be written in disappearing ink that only you can make reappear, so be it. If you want your journal to be covered in lipstick kisses or if you want it on your hard drive, describe it that way.

If you get bored during the writing of your letter, redouble your effort to talk directly as you would to a friend when describing a favorite article of clothing. Intensify your effort to fully visualize, audio-ize, olfact-ize and texture-ize. Use details and specifics. Be silly for a while, then serious, then nostalgic and fanciful, too.

I will share letters by some of my students so you can see theirs, but before you read them, try your hand at a letter.

ΙᎯᏅ

Now that you've written your account of what you envision your journal to be like, you'll probably enjoy hearing what others had to say:

MARA DAVIS'S JOURNAL

Dear Journal-to-Be:

My dream journal is like my house—a small, cozy, comfy multicolored spot to tuck away my prayers and thoughts and dreams. The cover is soft and square like a chenille pillow. It is bright pink to stimulate and inspire the senses. I like to caress its softness, imagining the tranquillity and comfort it will provide when I open it and begin to write.

It is glitter-sprinkled like stars in the night. Gold and silver glitter adorns the cover. Each page is a different color like the pillows stacked upon my sofa. There are hues of aqua, yellow, purple, mauve and blue. When I finish writing, I will sprinkle all of the pages with gold, silver, pink and purple glitter.

The journal is not too large, about thirty pages. Just small enough to fit inside my purse and carry wherever I go. The paper is off-white, not pure and somewhat stiff so that I can easily draw on it as well as write. The texture is important. I don't want a flimsy paper to carry my dreams.

And as for the final page, it is yellow and warm, a little like the rising sun, to mark a page that does not finish the book, but heralds the beginning of a brand new day and many more pages to come.

BARBARA FURNISS'S JOURNAL

Dear Journal-to-Be:

Many years ago my daughter gave me a small bound journal. Its unlined pages are only about a third full now, but I continue to keep it on a shelf by my bed, seldom making an entry, but telling myself that I will do so soon. It is handsome with its dark blue cover that borders an exotic black-and-white Escher print called *Three Worlds*.

Why don't I use it more? Perhaps it is too intimidating. I feel I must record noteworthy, wise observations, or else burble on with happy reflections. Maybe that is just an excuse, although I believe I am more comfortable with something less permanent. I want to be able to rip out pages and crumple them noisily in satisfying disgust before throwing them into the ever-waiting wastebasket. Baskets full of waste. I need to rethink this journal. It must be practical, but inviting. Not intimidating, but not too readily disposable so that I don't thoughtlessly throw away the substance of my life.

A hard look at my home work space provided the clues. My shelves are cluttered with notecards, pictures, scraps of paper that I cannot bear to throw away. The collection changes with the time of year, reflecting the season's activities and events. A zippered notebook with pockets would help.

I found it! Zippered, not too big, not too small with a spiral-bound book of lined paper inside. There are pockets on the inside cover as well as yellow stiff paper pockets at intervals in the lined insert. It is not as romantic as I would have liked—it is bound in businesslike dark green cloth and brown leather. I had envisioned a flowered cloth cover and rainbow shades of paper. But this one can travel with me, and I can crumple and throw away to my heart's content without violating its sturdy promise. When something wise materializes on its plain lined pages, who knows, I might even think about transferring it to the waiting, white pages of the Escher journal.

৩৩

After reading these two letters, think about our own writing. Were you detailed enough in your letter? Do you feel like you short-changed your journal by not giving it enough to go on? Go back into your letter and flesh things out if you feel like it. You will begin to get the hang of just how much detail helps you keep writing and expressing what it is you have to say.

Putting the Journal Together

To be an effective journal keeper, in addition to having some idea of how you want to go about things, you need to be cognizant of what roles you want your journal to fulfill.

I have read about people who called their journals a cri de coeur, a confidante, a listener, a therapist, a dream catcher, a bridge to self and a skylight.

I was thinking about this list when I heard Jorie Graham read her poems on the University of Arizona campus. She read a love poem in which she addresses her lover as "my love, my archive." I knew immediately that the list of all a journal can be was longer: file cabinet, family tree, growth hormone, taxidermist, soul mate, mirror, chair, track to run, mountain to hike, tree to sit under, ocean to dive into, cove to snorkel, sky to fly in, telephone to call myself, postal service, savings account, checking account, Medicaid, hospital, doctor, nurse, nutritionist, shaman, place of worship, collector of charitable donations.

Now it's your turn. Pick your favorite from my list or add one of your own. You are going to write a poem to your new journal with a strategy I borrowed from Pablo Neruda. He wrote "I Name You Queen," a beautiful poem in which he addresses his love saying there are lovelier, there are taller, and there are purer than she. He says no one else sees her crown and the carpet of gold at her feet when she walks by. But when he sees her, he is stirred and the world is filled with hymns and bells. He ends his poem with three short lines: "Only you and I,/only you and I my love,/Listen to it."

At the top of a page in your journal or as a first line in a paragraph, write "I name you _____" (fill in the term you chose). Tell your journal all the ways she is not the most superlative among those called by the same word or words. Tell her all the things you see in her that bespeak the name you have given her. And finally continue with a description of what happens inside you as a consequence of her existence.

Here are samples of writing to a journal about her name:

AMY JO GREENE'S "I NAME YOU" EXERCISE

I Name You

Today I name you JoMama. JoMama's Journal.

There are more creatively catchy titles to give you. There are easier
   names to call you.

There are no lesser pages of value in my house than you.

There are thousands of collections of my words lost without titles.

And there are journals with more wholeness of Amy or Jo.

But you are the new journal in the family of my writing life.

JoMama just seems to fit.

No one else sees the calm breeze you will cast across my hands.

No one else hears the words bounce like vivid multicolor hizzy tizzy fits on these BLUE blue college-ruled lines.

No one else touches the voids of emptiness like you will with your pages spilling over with me. My world.

And whenever I write in you, I will find the me who is lost in days filled with the unexpected.

Whenever I touch you, I will feel relaxed as I smooth the wrinkles from your pages never worrying of your judgment.

Whenever I pick you up, I will fill you with me and ecstatically come back to you again.

MARLEE MILLMAN'S "I NAME YOU" EXERCISE

I Name You Recorder of Feelings:

There are prettier ones than you.

There are better written ones than you.

There are funnier ones than you.

But you are my soul.

You let me rant and rave.

You let me feel sad or happy.

You never judge me.

You let me be.

No one else hears the despair.

No one else knows exactly what I think, except you, my recorder.

And whenever I read you, I see growth, I see change, I see pain.

But I also see contentment, good thoughts. It's a never ending process with you and I'm glad you are with me.

What Your Journal Is Made Of

What is your journal made of? You may decide that what you wrote in your Dear Journal-to-Be letter has a practical manifestation, or you may decide to keep it as a guiding metaphor only. I have had students who decided their journals needed fine leather covers to express their importance and some who have decided filing three by five cards suited them well. I have had students insist on spiral-bound notebooks from the supermarket so they wouldn't feel intimidated. I have used small legal pads because I like to write on them and a three-hole punch so I could put the papers in a three-ring binder. If your journal is not a spiral notebook or blank book, is it a pad, a calendar, loose-leaf paper, a scrapbook, a photo album with slots that writing as well as photos can fit into? Is it an in-and-out box, a plastic jug filled with letters to yourself? Now is the time to decide on a physical form for your journal, and to put it together. If your ideas are metaphorical, paste in pictures or include sketches in your journal to represent the metaphor.

Adding in Extras
Mad Money

When I started dating, my mother always made sure I had a dime with me—"mad money," she called it. A dime bought you a phone call at the nearest telephone booth, which was all it took, she said, if I felt uncomfortable with my date and needed a ride home. However, I always wanted the term *mad money* to mean I could do something really crazy if I wanted.

Money represents an exchange of energy. People's efforts and know-how are converted into currency (as in a flowing river) with which they purchase the fruits of other people's labor. Unfortunately, in life it is not as simple as that. We have been taught attitudes toward money ranging from the difficulty of obtaining enough of it to the idea that money equates with status and dictates our worth in more than financial ways. Depending on our backgrounds, we may feel that money represents a reservoir or we may think of it as a stream that can dry up. We may feel there is lots of time to make money or that time is money. Having money may seem the root of all evil or the best thing that can happen to us. In addition to these learned or adopted feelings and attitudes, we all have experienced disappointment or encouragement in situations involving money.

Whatever your history with money, put some kind of money in the front of your journal and write about why you chose what you did. You will find your choice has meaning for the journey ahead.

One woman in my class pasted a dollar to the cover of her journal. She told us a story about how when she was about eight, she wanted to be an artist. Her uncle said if she could draw a picture of a cow that looked like a cow, he would pay her one dollar. She worked hard at the drawing and when she was done, she presented the drawing to her uncle. "That doesn't look like a cow," he said. "You don't deserve this dollar." And he didn't give it to her. "Now," she said, "I'm paying myself in advance because everything I enter in my journal will be good enough and worthy."

Another student put foreign currency from Spain, Holland and Bulgaria in her journal. "I have worked so long in international finance that I know how to convert these currencies into the currency of many countries. In my journal, though, I want to write what I don't know yet. I am willing to enter into the mystery."

Someone else also found foreign currency for her journal and taped it into the inside cover because foreign currency makes her feel as if she is traveling.

Another journal had a penny taped into it. This journal keeper remembered how in early grade school she and her friends would pick up pennies they found on the ground and be delighted with the treasure until older kids made fun of them. "Oh, you still stoop for pennies. What a baby." It was no longer a pleasure to find this simple treasure. She either had to walk by pretending she didn't care or hope no one saw her pick the penny up. Either way the fun and excitement went out of the sudden discovery of a penny lying by her feet. This journal keeper didn't want to outgrow the innocence of being delighted.

Another journal keeper was given a fake million dollar bill laminated in plastic. Having it in her journal with the question of whether million dollar bills existed at all was motivating to her. And one more journal keeper put a quarter in her journal because that is how much a phone call was to stay in touch with others in her rural community when she was growing up.

Epigraphs

It is good to have an epigraph for your journal—a saying; a line from a song; a prayer; a poem; a quote from an author, actor or someone you know; or the fortune from a Chinese fortune cookie. Any line or lines you chose will help you connect your being with your wish to keep a journal. Inserting an epigraph is like christening a boat by hitting the neck of a champagne bottle against the bow. It's congratulations and the wish for a safe journey all in one. It's an emotional and philosophical jumping-off place. Don't worry about finding the perfect quote; find or choose one that has already come along in your life.

Here's a sentence that I have used from Dorothy Randall Gray's *Soul Between the Lines: Freeing Your Creative Spirit Through Writing*:

> There is a trickling of time in my life, a cascading
> mountain stream of moments that connect each spring
> and fall, each blossoming and harvest.
> —Daneen Perry

If you can't decide on only one quote for an epigraph, put in several. Here are some more I'm fond of:

How do islands float? Who invented shoes? Were shoes invented before cars?

—Austin Killien, second grade

. . . if the poet's subject be judiciously chosen, it will naturally, and upon fit occasion, lead him to passions the language of which, if selected truly and judiciously must necessarily be dignified and variegated, and alive with metaphors and figures.

—William Wordsworth

I get to recall where the romance of rock collecting had lain: the symbolic sense that underneath the dreary highways, underneath Pittsburgh, were canyons of crystals—that you could find treasure by prying open the landscape.

—Annie Dillard

When Mara Davis put together her journal created from the Dear Journal-to-Be letter, she used a paper book she had made in a book-making class. On the first page, she glued a collage that she had made from magazine cutouts. She said she had chosen pictures that stirred her. The quote she put inside the front cover, "Nobody cries in the ice cream shop," were words she had heard a proprietor speak to a little girl. She taped a penny inside because it represented the story of her father coming to this country with nothing and building a prosperous business. Of course she wanted her journal, empty at the start, to build into a lot, but she said this penny also represented that underneath everything (the hardships), you go on.

Exploring Issues of Privacy

Now that you have written a few pages for your journal, you are probably thinking about privacy. How can you keep your journal safe so certain people don't see it? This is a tricky question to answer. So much depends on the circumstances of the journal keeper: Who do they live with? Who comes to visit or care for things in their house? How respectful are those people?

It is not that hard or expensive to get or create a locking box and keep it under a bed or desk. It is not that hard to install a locking doorknob on a closet. It is not that hard to find file cabinets with drawers that lock. If knowing you can keep your journal out of reach creates peace of mind, I suggest you make a safe place to keep the journal where you will not worry about intruding eyes coming upon your words and thoughts.

If you are worried about being associated with your journal, you can always title the book and create a pen name for its author: "My Book of Days," "Between the Dishes and the Dog Food," "Journey to a New River" or "Journey to Writing Country" all appeal to me. Then create your own pen name and put "by _____" under your title. Even if you don't mind having your name on your journal, creating a title for the book seems a nice touch.

Do not feel odd if you want to share your journals and have others listen to sections or read sections for themselves. There are many people working with journals today in groups that listen to entries by everyone. The Transcendentalists shared their journals— Emerson, Thoreau and their writing buddies looked forward to their group meetings in which they discussed the nature of journal writing as well as their actual journal entries. When you share entries, ask the people to respond in a particular way: ask them to first tell you back memorable phrases and words. It is your entry they are hearing. Too often people use one person's work as a springboard to talk about themselves; this is not real listening. The journal above all is a place of listening closely to the world, both outer and inner, and it will feel like a real violation if someone listens to your entry and skips over this step of letting you know they *listened*. After they tell you what they heard, ask them how they felt after hearing it. Encourage them to think of lots of names for their feelings: angry, sad, disappointed, encouraged, joyful, happy, excited, eager, anticipatory, stimulated, motivated, protected, hidden, revealed, curious, surprised, threatened, connected, alienated, hungry, sated, lightened, burdened, forgetful, alert, wistful, nostalgic—these are only a handful of words that describe feelings. Hearing your readers label their feelings may help you know more about what your concerns and interests are. If you desire, ask them to talk about memories or situations your writing made them think about.

Exploring Issues of Commitment

Most important is your *commitment* to keeping this journal. According to *Webster's II New Riverside University Dictionary*, commitment means "the state of being bound emotionally or intellectually to an ideal or course of action." *Emotionally or intellectually* are good words for the journal keeper to fuse. To keep a journal requires both an emotional and cognitive desire. A journal keeper feels pleased and almost propelled to use writing as a way of thinking. A journal keeper gets emotional pleasure from the process of thinking in writing and receives information about her life during the process of journaling and self-reflection on the journal entries.

It is one thing, though, to know you need commitment, and quite another to have or develop such a thing. Most of us begin by behaving as if we did have the commitment, felt the compulsion, had to continue. By acting "as if," we help ourselves toward authentically feeling that way. I once read that for some action to become a habit, one must repeat that action about twenty-one consecutive times. After those twenty-one times, the behavior becomes habitual and there is no resistance to doing it. So, if you are going to write daily, you have only twenty-one days of "as ifing" it, and if you are going to do things weekly or somewhere in between daily and weekly, you have a longer stretch of "as ifing." Each time you sit down to write in the journal, do something that helps you feel delighted to be writing in your journal. This might be accompanying the journal writing with a favorite cup of tea or coffee, listening to your favorite music as you write, or promising yourself a long phone conversation with a friend when you have completed your entry. You might also combine journal keeping with an activity you already do habitually and enjoy. You could write journal entries during a bicycle trip by keeping a pen and notebook in your bike bag and stopping to write along the route or just when you have completed it. This holds true for those of you who take long walks. Maybe you like to park your car by the ocean or a lake or a favorite park and watch the people or the birds. Take your notebook and pen along. Combining your journal keeping with other pleasure time might keep you building a commitment to both of them.

Another factor in developing commitment is the feeling of competency. When we feel we are doing well at a task it is easier to stay committed to doing that task. It is not that the task is easy, but that we are capable of facing its difficulties and continuing. The exercises that follow are all ones you will feel able to complete. Even if you can't tell immediately what new things you have learned about yourself, you will feel as if you have written fully and well. When it comes time to use the self-reflection questions offered at the end of each quarter of journaling, you will discover more about what your writing is revealing about your goals, desires and core feelings.

Yet another factor in the development of commitment is our belief that remaining with something or someone will help us develop into better human beings because our development feeds theirs and theirs feeds ours. It is possible to develop such a relationship with your journal. The journal prompts you to speech and becomes a nonjudgmental listener; in turn, the journal grows rich in recorded experience.

Finally, to keep commitment alive, we have to believe in what we are going to gain from this commitment. In keeping a journal, I value gaining a listener, gaining a confidante who will prompt me to speak from my own voice and gaining a colleague in moving through the flow of time.

I want to help you understand and accept rather than run from any feelings that subvert your commitment. Anyone writing is likely at times to feel amateurish. No one wants to feel that way when it comes to something as important as writing the journey into oneself. One of my students made me promise I would address the feelings that make people feel inadequate to write in their own journals. This seems like just the place.

We sometimes come to the page afraid of what we might see in print, afraid that what we feel may be transitory but made frighteningly permanent in ink. We are afraid that we don't have the right to say what we might say in our writing. We are afraid that our observations are unimportant in the scheme of things, even to ourselves. We are afraid we might sound petty or whiney or close-minded or uninformed or dull. Or we may fear we'll discover that something is close to the surface that we wish had already been laid to rest. I know no better way to calm these fears than to say that you must write through them. What keeps me going and keeps me from being trapped by issues of tone or disenfranchisement, is my belief in the power of sensory detail to keep me aware of myself and the way I see, hear, taste, touch and smell things. Whenever I resort to detail that comes in through the senses, I feel empowered to write my experience. I don't feel alarmed that I am judging because the images speak for themselves. I learn from my words.

I have a friend who cried watching a particular scene in the film *City of Angels* in which an immortal played by Nicolas Cage is in love with a mortal played by Meg Ryan. The immortal who comes to Earth has no sense of taste since he is not a creature of the Earth. The mortal is cutting a pear. Nicolas Cage asks Meg Ryan what a pear tastes like. She laughs, saying a pear tastes like a pear. He says something like, "I mean what does a pear taste like to you?" My friend was moved by the insistence in this interchange that each of us experience uniquely and communicate what our senses tell us.

ↂ

How can you help yourself believe in your journal keeping and take it seriously enough to continue? Let's start in the next chapter with an approach that builds your ideas of your own competence and helps you truly encourage a solid working relationship with your journal.

CHAPTER FOUR

Hiring the Journal Keeper Within

> . . . the heart . . . and the learned skills of the conscious
> mind . . . make appointments with each other, and keep
> them, and something begins to happen.
>
> MARY OLIVER
> *A Poetry Handbook*

Years ago when I was helping my husband start a computer net-
working training and consulting business, he and I attended a time
management seminar put on by the Day-Timer people. I thought
I managed my time very well since I was working for my husband,
teaching, raising kids and writing. I believed my purpose for going
was so my husband would go. But I learned something that day
that has helped me ever since. Using an overhead projector, the
presenter showed us someone's system of keeping personal and job
to-do lists in separate places. He then showed us what it would look
like if the person just kept it all together in one book. He said we
waste time and effort when we try to separate our lives according
to what is for work and what is personal. If you mean to call a
florist to send flowers to your wife for her birthday or you need to
make a doctor's appointment, you should put it right in the book
with the meetings to attend and memos to be written.

As a writer and teacher of writing, I was hearing a variation on
this theme—one of separation of work and trying to write almost
daily. If I wasn't saying it, someone I knew or was teaching was

saying: "If only I didn't have to work full time, then I could pay attention to my writing." "If only I wasn't raising toddlers (or school-age kids or teenagers), then I'm sure I'd do more writing." "If only I wasn't the one who has to do all the record keeping and bill paying and busy work in our household, then I'd write more." If only, if only, if only.

When the time management presenter talked about the time wastefulness of separating our lives this way, he struck a cord with me. He said it was all part of life and was supposed to be kept on the same page. I immediately thought to myself, hadn't William Carlos Williams and Wallace Stevens, two poets I had studied, worked as full-time professionals and still written—a lot? Hadn't I seen a video re-enactment in a series called *Visions and Voices* in which someone playing the poet William Carlos Williams finishes a house call to a sick patient and sits behind the steering wheel of his parked car writing a poem on a handy prescription pad? Hadn't I learned that Wallace Stevens walked to work as an insurance agent and on the way composed the lines of his poetry? Hadn't I learned that when it came to writing from the self, one had to combine time to write with the time it took to be in the world with all of its demands and cares?

I had, but I just hadn't done enough about it. I was a vacation-based writer, finding time to write in accordance with the school calendar. When I was not teaching, I'd spend consolidated time writing. Summer months were good writing months, and fall and spring months were more difficult for me. But after the Day-Timer talk, I wrote more during the months I worked and taught. I learned to clear space for myself and my writing on that piled-up desk of mine. When I couldn't manage to get the space I wanted that way, I learned to get it by driving a short distance away for an hour or less. I'd drive to a park, a scenic viewing spot along Puget Sound or sometimes just to a different block and sit behind my steering wheel and write a while.

I was interspersing hours of writing with hours of working and raising a family and keeping all of the associated tasks in time slots on the same daily to-do list. I was also changing my sensibility: I had hired myself, I realized, to do the work I really wanted done!

I offer the exercises in this chapter as a process by which you can hire yourself to do the journal keeping you want done. It is a process that helps build confidence that you are the right person for the job. And it is easier than you might think. Do these exercises directly in your journal, or if you wish, paste them in later.

Creating a Job Description That Works

When you have a position to be filled, you must engage in a hiring process. The first step to building an effective process is to write a job description that encapsulates the responsibilities, duties and functions of the person who will be hired. This is your chance to fully imagine the job you want done and to list the skills your hire will have.

Across the top of a page write the title "Position: Journal Keeper." For the next ten minutes, describe this job. What would the person you hire be called upon to do in this journal keeper position? What would you expect the functions of such a person to include? What skills would such an applicant need to convince you that he or she had? Remember, this is not just any journal keeper—this is YOUR journal keeper. This person might have to be able to write on the fly or be especially able to pick up midsentence with something he or she was writing a week ago. The job description depends upon what your life is like and what you need from the journal keeper. If you are hoping that the very existence in your life of this journal keeper will change the job into something more serene than it might be now, say this and describe what you are hoping for.

Since your job description won't show up in a want ad that costs by the word, take another ten or twenty minutes and write some anecdotal accounts of how you have come to know these are the functions, duties and skills required for the job of being your journal keeper. You didn't pull these notions out of thin air. They were born of your experiences, wishes and dreams. Write that down!

Here is a short job description done by Suzanne Willsey:

Job Title
Journal Keeper
Minimum Qualifications
Must have a passion for words, sense of humor, keen sense of observation. Must be a collector of images, willing to take risks and make time for the work.
Job Specifics
Hours and location: to be arranged by you
This job offers flexibility for the busy writer. It can be done in your car, at the dentist office, at the park, in a cafe or poolside. You set the time and place.
Compensation
If you are selected for this job, you will be compensated by a feeling of satisfaction and relief that the journal lives again— resurrected by the strength of your creativity and desire to write.
Inquire
Within

Janice Goodman wrote:
WANTED: Someone with a pen, a notebook, an imagination,

Someone who enjoys quiet,
Someone who enjoys conversation,
Someone who sees things just a little bit differently,
Someone who can paint pictures with words,
Someone who has something to say.

Letter of Introduction

Imagine someone responding to the job description you have written. In a letter, let the person speak in a natural but persuasive voice about why he or she is right for the job. The candidate may even be so bold as to add a few ideas of his or her own.

Here is an "ad" written by Barbara Furniss:

WANTED: A dedicated Journal Writer willing to engage in a long commitment. Personal physical attributes of no importance, but must be reliable to the point of doggedness. Applicant should anticipate excitement and satisfaction as rewards for participating in this relationship. Send reasons for applying and provide E-mail address if possible.

Here is the accompanying letter from her applicant:

I am writing in response to your request for a Journal Writer, even though at my age (seventy-seven) I am a shade nervous about what you call a "long commitment." My Dream Journal is in readiness. It is perfect for me: zippered so that pens, pictures and notes don't escape from the interior pockets; a lined removable notebook that can be replaced, and a small, safe pocket filled with colorful foreign money. Now I only have to put it to work. My Dream Journal is named Patient Friend, not exactly a jazzy name, but don't let that put you off, because patience and friendship are needed in this intimate relationship.

To be honest with you, this is my third try at applying for the job. The garbage truck almost got the first one before I exhumed it from my trash barrel. I guess I was worried about it being too idealistic, but here goes:

I am willing to commit to frequent, regular entries in my journal.

I am convinced that this commitment will be freeing rather than constraining.

I believe it will lead to greater creativity in all aspects of my life, including writing.

My journal entries will provide a time for listening to myself, and will act as a corrective to distorted memories.

I will carry the concept of journaling throughout the day, savoring special moments, places and events so that my journal record becomes a mosaic of a rightly experienced life.

My second application will not be included here. It reflects my growing infatuation with my Dream Journal which is downright embarrassing because we spend a lot of time in bed together.

I still subscribe to the sentiments in my first application, but I am learning to make my journal reflect more closely life as I observe it each day. My entries can include something as simple as a correctly remembered party recipe, a quotation that I want to save, the feel of my cat when she uses my leg as a prop while bathing, my dismay at learning that a good friend is not healing well after a nasty operation, or just anything. I like that: just anything!

Interviewing the Candidate

It is often overwhelming to meet and interview candidates for a job, and it is usually quite overwhelming to be the candidate having the interview.

The interviewer wonders, "Did I make the impression I was a skillful manager? Did I ask the right questions for really learning about the prospective employee? Did I describe the job and its duties accurately enough that the candidate really knows what I am looking for?"

The candidate wonders, "Did I dress appropriately? Did I mumble, or did I project my voice confidently? Did I seem intelligent and give the impression that I understood the job and what it requires? Did I seem like someone who could both take directions and work independently as a self-starter? Did I ask the kind of questions bosses like to hear, the ones that show I am thoughtful but focused?"

You get to have fun here. Write an exchange between you, the hiring agent, and you, the job applicant. You can do this all in dialogue, or you can add inner thoughts and asides on both characters' parts. Fully visualize where and when this interview is taking place so details of the environment and time of day can be included in the characters' thoughts and words.

On an episode of the TV show *ER*, Carrie Weaver, the head resident in the emergency room, is interviewing for the position of a head doctor. A warmhearted but inappropriate clerk on the floor says of Carrie's outfit something like, "Oh, you read that magazine article, too—the one about what to wear when you are interviewing for the important position!" Later in the episode, another woman candidate is dressed similarly and we know for sure Carrie did in fact read that article.

This is the kind of thing you can write into your dialogue. The interviewer might comment on the applicant's attire or either party might have thoughts about the other's or her own clothing. Either party might comment on the surroundings where they are interviewing or the place where the job is assigned. Let yourself have fun putting two human beings in this conversation that is actually wholly off the record.

Designate a Start Date and Place of Employment

Pretend that you are talking to your new employee over the phone or writing a letter or an E-mail to her making the offer of employment. If you have any reservations at this time or areas of concern you want your new employee to know you will be watching and evaluating, get these off your chest in this conversation or message. When you have written this exchange or correspondence, end it by stating the start date, the start time and the place your new hire is to report. Be sure to tell the employee how many times per week you expect her to write in the journal, where and when to report to work. Are her hours and the location she works from flexible or more structured? Be sure she understands how to use the journal you have created and want kept. Write this all down.

How to Proceed Using the Next Chapters

You have worked hard to envision this job well and to conjure the journal keeper you have hired. Now it's the journal keeper's turn to work. In the chapters to come, there will be plenty of work to keep your new hire happy, whether her hours are daily or only weekly to start.

Whenever you start is week one. The year is divided into four quarters of thirteen weeks each. Chapter five has the first quarter exercises, chapter six the second quarter, chapter seven the third quarter and chapter eight the fourth quarter. The exercises for each week in all the quarters include six extensions so the person who wants to write every day will have a prompt for every day. If you write less than daily, you can pick and chose among the extensions. The creative writing ideas for the entries help you find structures and strategies that invite writing. The thirteenth week of each quarter has a week's worth of self-reflection exercises meant to help you review your work and gain insight.

Leaving the self-reflection journal exercises for the week following three months of writing helps you write each week without worrying about the deeper meaning of your entries. The momentum of writing without worrying about what the writing is revealing about its author is important. Taking time to contemplate what the writing is telling and what the writing is keeping from telling is something you can best evaluate after a bulk of entries have been made. At that point, it becomes a pleasure to look over the writing because there is so much there.

In addition to the weekly writing ideas, there are special exercises in chapter nine to use as substitutes during special weeks or days of your journaling year. There are exercises for days or weeks with losses or renewals in the form of breakups, deaths, births and other new beginnings. And there are exercise ideas for writing on holidays. Look these exercises over so you are familiar with them. Then when a holiday or special occasion turns up, you will know what special exercise you might want to substitute that day or week.

Troubleshooting

If a particular week's writing ideas are not inspiring you, don't let the writing go. You can always freewrite for entries about subjects of your own choosing. To do this, give yourself a specific amount of time to write (using an oven timer or beeper is helpful). Put a pen in your hand and just keep it moving across the pages as you write whatever you feel like writing (putting in plenty of sensory detail, of course) for the whole time you have allotted. You can also always do any of the extensions from a previous week that you didn't choose the first time or that you feel like repeating. The intention in this book is to help you keep writing for a year. If using the weekly and daily writing ideas is always useful, go ahead and keep using them. If you need a break at times from this structure, feel free to supply a structure of your own or use the freewriting approach until you're ready to use writing ideas as springboards. If you want to write about special occasions for longer than a day or a week, feel free to borrow from the ideas in chapter nine many days in a row.

Be sure you are writing in sentences and paragraphs. Sometimes inertia sets in and it is possible to make quick lists of images and thoughts. Some exercises are in the form of litanies, but even in these exercises that are lists, the length and detail in the sentences creates the thinking. Take the time to write fully or you will be shortchanging the thinking that is done in writing.

And always remember, the physical form of this journal is up to you. Whether you keep a notebook, computer files or a box or cabinet full of your writing, it is still a journal. I do think you will want to date the entries so you can tell when you wrote them, even if your system doesn't require you to store things in chronological order. A notation like "Week One: Wednesday, August 9, 2000" may come in handy. For instance, if you keep photographs with dates you can later match images with writing.

For more journaling after this first year, you can reuse the chapters. The prompts and exercise ideas are not meant to be answered only one way and only once. I hope you will enjoy many seasons of keeping your journal. To help you with this, I have also included a chapter with information on resources for the continuing journal keeper.

∽∾∽

But now, let's get that new worker started. Turn the page and it is week number one!

CHAPTER FIVE

First Quarter

I see that my neighbors look with compassion on me, that
they think it is a mean and unfortunate destiny which makes
me walk in these fields and woods so much and sail on this
river alone. But so long as I find here the only real elysium,
I cannot hesitate in my choice.

HENRY DAVID THOREAU

OCTOBER 18, AGE 39

Whenever we start something new it is a time of returning, like
children to school in the fall when there are new teachers, classrooms, classmates, textbooks, notebooks and clubs to join. With all
the newness there is one thing familiar—the concern about doing
it right. We are used to asking ourselves with worry, "Will people
like me?" "Will I be able to do the work?" "Will I get chosen to
be on the team?" Concerns like these cause us to be self-conscious.
One of the many forms this self-consciousness takes when we write
is a vicious comparing and self-editing. "If only I could write like
that," we may lament after reading or hearing someone's writing
and then decide that the "if only" means we can't. Or we worry
about our ability to write at all because we have trouble spelling or
writing grammatically or punctuating our sentences correctly. Even
though we know none of this should matter as we write in our own
journals, it is hard to eradicate those many red pencil strokes we

are used to seeing on our words and the remembered grimace the teacher made as she corrected papers.

Since we want to bring a lot of feeling and emotion to the act of writing, we are sad experiencing the discrepancy between our desire to share some of ourselves on the page and the discomfort we felt when errors in our presentation were pointed out. We shrink from the situation and many of us to this day cannot sit down to write as comfortably as we may speak. How sad that one of the best ways we have to communicate with ourselves—thinking through writing, making leaps of imagination and association to find our true thoughts and feelings—is contaminated with the imposed idea that how we do something is more important than what we are attempting to do.

Luckily, we can muster some power over these voices and images from the past through exercises in our journal. As you start in this first three months of journaling, you will work on some journal writing ideas that build your confidence in your own voice, desires and ways of looking at the world.

WEEK ONE
Dialogues to Diffuse the Power of Critical Voices

One morning I was flying Southwest Airlines from Seattle to Tucson where I was going to teach a weekend writing class. Southwest Airlines gives boarding passes at the gate, first come, first serve, and then they load their planes in boarding groups rather than assigning particular seats to passengers. The boarding passes are given out one hour before departure, and people start lining up earlier than that before the agent has actually arrived at the counter. In line that morning, I was standing behind an elderly man and a middle-aged man, both dressed in western gear—tight jeans, cowboy boots and cowboy hats, their belt buckles sparkling under the fluorescent light-

ing. They may have been father and son. Their conversation went
something like this:

OLDER MAN: There sure were a lot people downstairs at the
check-in.

YOUNGER MAN: Yup, these days, you can never give yourself
enough time.

OLDER MAN: They sure wanted us here early and there's no one
ready to see us.

YOUNGER MAN: Yup, that's how it is, hurry up and wait.

OLDER MAN: I guess we could've gotten all jammed up at that
place where they check the carry-ons and the people for
weapons.

YOUNGER MAN: Yup, these days you can't have enough security.

On the plane preparing for my class, I found that the conversation I had overheard was inspiring a writing idea. The use of cliches
and overused knee-jerk reaction sentences by the younger man kept
the conversation from going anywhere. I could ask people to think
of an area in their lives where they used to or now have to interact
with someone they feel has annoying power over them. I could
suggest they write a dialogue with that person in which the person
says what they usually say, but the writer answers in cliches. This
would have the effect of diffusing that power, of keeping it from
going anywhere. The results from this exercise were funny and freeing. And this is what your first week's journaling exercise is because
it will help you take power:

1. Think of a place or situation in which someone has power
over you that you find annoying.

2. Name your journal entry after this place or situation: Talking
to the Head of the Board of Directors in the Board Room;

At Lunch With My Mother; When My Teenage Son Comes Down From His Room.

3. Write a dialogue in which the annoyingly powerful person speaks the way they normally do and you reply to each line of theirs with a cliche. Don't worry about how the cliche fits. Just write down whatever cliches pop into your head after you've written the other person's lines.

You may want to do a dialogue like this for yourself before reading and enjoying the following samples. But if you need to peek at the samples, go ahead. I wrote about my inner critic:

CRITIC: Everything you write is dull.

ME: Well, a bird in the bush is worth two in the hand.

CRITIC: Really, I mean it, your images are not interesting.

ME: Monkey see, monkey do.

CRITIC: You always got Bs in composition, not As. You're just not that good.

ME: Don't judge a book by its cover.

CRITIC: And you write so short, why not a novel? Why always essays and poems?

ME: Well, good things come in small packages.

CRITIC: You're using cliches, you know, and that's a big no-no for a writer.

ME: A stitch in time saves nine.

Here Marjorie Hilts, another journal keeper, conjures this conversation with her cat:

GAY: I can't think why you would want me to go outside just because you plan to leave.

ME: Because I say so and I'm the boss.

GAY: But I'm afraid of the javelinas (desert animal in Tucson).

ME: The only thing you have to fear is fear itself.

GAY: What if they chase me?

ME: Just tuck your tail between your legs and run.

GAY: How come I always have to do what you want?

ME: I'm bigger than you.

GAY: But I'm prettier.

ME: Pretty is as pretty does.

GAY: You're so mean to me.

ME: Pouting will get you nowhere.

GAY: If you loved me you wouldn't make me go outside.

ME: Spare the rod and spoil the child.

GAY: You'll be sorry when the coyotes get me.

ME: If you love someone, let him go.

Any time we capture our resistance to feeling pushed around, we are helping to free ourselves from the forces that trample our desire to express ourselves. Try your hand at such a dialogue.

SIX EXTENSIONS OF THIS EXERCISE

1. Choose others who, annoyingly, also have power over you and write dialogues between them and yourself similar to the one you did previously.

2. Take each cliche that you came up with in the dialogue or dialogues and do a freewrite for each about what meaning that cliche has for you, not only vis-à-vis the person you were responding to in the dialogue, but in other life situations, past and present.

3. Take your dialogue, or your favorite of the bunch if you've done more than one, and write a letter to the person you are

speaking with telling him or her how you feel now that you have had this "conversation."

4. Take one or more of the dialogues and describe the annoyingly powerful person in great detail. What do you see, hear, taste, touch and smell when you think of this person or persons?

5. Think of yourself in one or more of these dialogues. Describe yourself in detail. How old are you? How do you look? What are you thinking about? What is making you uncomfortable—a pebble in your shoe, an eyelash in your eye? What would you rather be doing? What does the person you are having to respond to remind you of? What would make you laugh thinking it quietly to yourself?

6. Think about the critic you hold in your head who is always judging you. Write a death scene for this critic. Where does it take place? What or who causes the death? How does the critic struggle? Why does the critic's struggle fail? What was the critic's Achilles' heel? The critic is dead and you are free! Write about that—how does it feel and how will you use this freedom?

WEEK TWO
A Lesson From Morrie and Rilke

After I had started writing this book, I read *Tuesdays With Morrie: An Old Man, a Young Man and the Last Great Lesson* by Mitch Albom, a narrative by a former college student of the last six months of his favorite professor's life. What is so inspiring in this account is the teacher's voice and thoughts as he prepares to die but must first finish what he is on this earth to do—teach what he has learned from his experience. His desire for connection and his pleasure in what connections come his way, particularly the small ones, made me, and I am sure most of the book's readers, tearful and appreciative.

Morrie tells his former student, "You can run up and down the block and go crazy. I can't do that. I can't go out. I can't run. . . . But you know what? I *appreciate* that window more than you do. . . . I look out that window every day. I notice the change in the trees, how strong the wind is blowing. It's as if I can see time actually passing through that windowpane." Morrie tells his student, "We are too involved in materialistic things, and they don't satisfy us. The loving relationships we have, the universe around us, we take these things for granted."

These words make me think of the poet Rilke. In *Letters to a Young Poet*, he writes of Italy:

> . . . no, there is not more beauty here than elsewhere, and all these objects, continuously admired by generations and patched and mended by workmen's hands, signify nothing, are nothing, and have no heart and no value;—but there is much beauty here, because there is much beauty everywhere. . . . Through such impressions one collects oneself, wins oneself back again out of the pretentious multiplicity that talks and chatters there (and how talkative it is!), and one learns slowly to recognize the very few things in which the eternal endures that one can love and something solitary in which one can quietly take part.

Reread aloud the last two lines of the paragraph above: ". . . and one learns slowly to recognize the very few things in which the eternal endures that one can love and something solitary in which one can quietly take part."

Adopt a window or a place outside where you will record your observations right now and again during your journal keeping process. The eternal, no doubt, endures in all places, but there are very few, Rilke tells us, that any one of us can love deeply. He tells us it is something solitary in which we take part when we recognize these few places. Morrie looks out one window and appreciates it.

Sit awhile at your adopted window or outdoor place. Jot down what you see, hear, feel, smell and even taste or remember with your senses because you are sitting in this spot now. Imagine yourself director of your own short film on your adopted place. What does the camera select for the viewer to see—people and their activities, plants, animals, man-made technologies and buildings? What small things will the camera zoom in on? Where will the camera pan? Who walks on screen? What ambient sounds are on the soundtrack? Now that the scene is evoked, let someone or something suddenly fill up the camera's lens. Anyone or anything that pops into your mind can pop into this scene. People, pets and objects are sometimes where we recognize the eternal and our connection to it.

In your writing become the voice-over in a documentary. Ask this figure why it has come and what it is getting from the scene. Write down the answer you "heard." For example, I might write, "When I asked my grandfather why he was up from his grave now walking outside my window on this September day, he looked toward the clouds and I had to walk in the direction he was looking to record his voice. He began to tell me. . . ."

SIX EXTENSIONS OF THIS EXERCISE

1. Go to the same window or place many times and start again describing the scene until someone or something pops up before the lens. If it is the same person or thing, write more of what they have come to tell you.

2. Pretend you are enlarging one part of the scene outside your window or in your place. Describe what you are enlarging.

What do you see now that the object or person is bigger? Write for ten minutes on what is revealed with the enlargement. You can begin, "Until I magnified what I was looking at, I didn't . . . but now I see. . . ."

3. Imagine a blind person in the scene you have written about. Write the scene from their point of view.

4. "Because I know my time is almost done," Morrie says in the book *Tuesdays With Morrie*, "I am drawn to nature like I'm seeing if for the first time." Since you have only a short time to look out your adopted window or be in your adopted outdoor spot, you can use this idea of limited time forcing you to see. Write a litany about the scene from your adopted place where each line starts with the words "Because I know my time is almost done." Each line continues with something you observe through the senses—e.g., "Because I know my time is almost done, I taste the cherries from the tree and let the purple juice drip down my chin. Because I know my time is almost done, I touch the earth as if it were the skin of a little boy's scraped knee." Now it's your turn: "Because I know my time is almost done, I. . . ."

5. Practice making similes as you look and experience your spot. What are you seeing, hearing, tasting, touching and smelling that you can compare to other sights, sounds, tastes, textures and smells and sensations? "The tall row of poplar trees are like Vikings coming to this land. The smell of newly baked bread wafting from the bakery is like my small son's skin when it's warmed by the sun. The sound of the church bells ringing is like pennies falling from my childhood piggy bank. Wind between the buildings pushes at me like my mother behind the swing when I was young. The smell of the first tulips in springtime is like the smell of new oil crayons for

art class." Take over now and make a litany of similes from your experience of your spot.

6. If you were going to be moving and had only one more time to be at your spot, what would you do instead of writing? Take pictures for an album? Describe the pictures you'd have for the album. Make a bouquet? What would you gather for the bouquet? Talk with people or animals that are there? Who are they and what would you be talking about? Choose an activity and write about yourself doing it in that location.

WEEK THREE
Letter to a Columnist

I have always, it seems, been a reader of letters to Ann Landers. I like to read the column in *Parade Magazine* in which teens write about their concerns and other teens respond with what they feel and think. Some of the most useful letters in any of these columns are from people who have experienced something particular about human nature or the human condition firsthand.

For this week's exercise, write a letter to Ann Landers or a local columnist concerning an issue you would like to inform others about. The person who understands that a teenage son having trouble waking in the morning may not be merely "lazy," the person whose loved one has been hospitalized and now understands the importance of the staff listening to the patient, the young woman who was unable to cope with being diagnosed with diabetes and now understands how to cope and why it is important—these are the kind of people who have useful things to say to others. But also, by writing they get to experience their wisdom.

You might want to start with the clustering technique I introduced in chapter three to gather ideas about what areas in your life have provided the opportunities for the kind of wisdom you can share in a letter. Put the words "firsthand experience" in the center of a blank piece of paper and begin clustering all the categories of firsthand experience you have had—dating, parenting, marrying, supervising, being supervised, fixing machines, painting houses, aiding the sick or dying, public speaking, teaching preschool, etc. Let yourself cluster around the categories that come up. In the back of your mind keep the idea that you have learned something from at least one of these experiences that you want to put into words. Soon you will feel a particular interest in one of the categories. Stop clustering and begin your letter, which written out of firsthand experience allows you to find out what your experience has taught you.

SIX EXTENSIONS OF THIS EXERCISE

1. Think about who in your own life most needs the information in your letter. Write another letter directly to this person telling why you want her to know what you are writing. How do you feel writing this information to this person? What are you hoping she will do as a consequence of having this information? Do you want to hear back from this correspondent? Why or why not? Include the answers to these questions in the body of this letter.

2. Think about what people might write to the columnist as a consequence of seeing your letter in the paper. Write one or more of their letters back to the columnist in response to your letter.

3. Visualize years passing. The newsprint on which your letter was published is yellowed and brittle now. Someone two generations down in your family comes across your letter. She brings it to her parents' attention. Imagine her age and cir-

cumstances. Write the dialogue that ensues when she asks one or both of her parents about the letter you wrote so long ago.

4. Visualize this child further. Dress her, give her a place to live, siblings, cousins, children of her own, a career, a husband, pets, travels, dilemmas—whatever you feel like endowing her with. Let her write a letter to you telling you how the information in your letter affects her.

5. Imagine a copy of the newspaper in which the letter first appeared. What happens to that newspaper? Keep it somehow from getting dumped and burned. How does it travel from household to household and make it through the years? What chain of events determines where the paper is used and left? What value does the letter ultimately have even if only a paragraph or a sentence survives? Authors think like this and have organized whole books in this way. I think now of Annie Proulx's *Accordion Crimes*, organized around the idea of following a handmade accordion as it gets lost, stolen and traded over the years.

6. Write more letters. Pretend you are on a letter-writing frenzy and expect to have all of your letters printed without delay in newspaper columns.

WEEK FOUR
Reading, Writing and 'Rithmatic,
Taught to the Tune of What I Did

Let this week's exercise take you back to your school days. Instead of thinking about goals and learning, though, think about things you did that you are not really proud of. This may be one thread that connects everyone in school no matter which role they played—jokester, prom queen, nerd, jock or cheerleader.

When I thought of my early school years, I wrote the following poem:

Walking to School

At six, I walk to school with Jackie,
Jerry and Karen, our glass-lined thermoses
filled with milk, Roy Rogers and Dale Evans
smiling from our metal lunch boxes.

We decide to play Talk Like the Grown-Ups.
No one is allowed to finish their sentence.
It is hard cutting into friends' words, but we
keep slicing conversation all the way to the bridge.

A deformed girl, chin tight to her shoulders, crosses
ahead of us, piggybacking her sister. "No Neck!
There's No Neck again," we shout and run.
Then the girl's eyes meet mine.

I tighten my grip on my lunch box, trip,
the glass inside my thermos shattering. When I
get home, Mother pours the milk with its hundred
shiny slivers, each the eye of the morning girl,
each meeting my eyes out the porcelain sink forever.

My behavior is not behavior I am proud of and it is not the kind of behavior I like to write about. Nonetheless, it is what we did, my fellow kindergartners and me.

What behavior can you recount from your school years that you are not proud of? Write it out. You might begin, "I never told anybody about the time that. . . ." or "Only a few of us know about the time that . . ." or "Even though everybody knows this story, let me tell you the way I remember that day."

SIX EXTENSIONS OF THIS EXERCISE

1. Stories of misbehavior or mischief have victims. Write a letter from the victim to you, the perpetrator, telling you her feelings concerning the situation. She might be surprisingly funny on the subject and not nearly as angry as you think.

2. Put this story in another context or time. If it happened in school, write it as if it is happening in the workplace; if it happened in your old neighborhood write it as if its happening in the neighborhood you now live in. Replace the people with people from your present.

3. There must be many more things you are reluctant to tell others. In his instructional book, *I Never Told Anybody*, poet Kenneth Koch encourages senior citizens to write the many things that they have never told anybody. Many of these things do not involve mischief or inappropriate behavior but hopes and dreams and small pleasures. Think of a person you knew or know now that you never really liked too much. Do a "I Never Told Anybody" list from his or her point of view. For instance, the class wallflower could begin, "I never told anybody what I think when I stand there watching the boys ask other girls to dance. I never told anybody I think about the way chess pieces on a board advance and jump side to side. I never told anybody I think it would be better to be like the pawn who is taken off the board to sit at its edge. At least it could happen that a horse or a knight might join her and she could. . . ."

4. Have a superhero, religious figure or revered elder miracu-

lously enter the scene of your original story about misbehaving. Instead of preaching to you about good and noble ways to behave, let this figure tell you about what you will learn from this nastiness or trickiness or cruel judging. Since this figure can see the future, he or she can tell how what you did then taught you to behave a certain way later.

5. Set things right for the victim of your old behavior. Award her or him presents and explain the meaning of each gift. Think of small particular gifts—even silly things—and you will have an easier time addressing the subject than if you try to award big, impossible presents.

6. Write about a time you behaved surprisingly well. You could start, "I may be the same person who . . . , but there was also a time that I . . . ," or "I may be the same person who took part in the . . . , but today I am the person who. . . ."

WEEK FIVE
Cider Mills and Burning Leaves

In every season we do our chores and savor the treats of the season. For some, fall brings leaves to rake (and sometimes to burn) and cider mills to visit where we sip fresh apple cider and eat sweet doughnuts. Winter brings pipes to save from freezing, animals to protect from the cold, ice skating and tobogganing. Or in warm weather climates, winter brings visitors and lots of activity. Spring brings gardens to sow and closets to go through. New bulbs are up and flowering. Summer brings longer days, more leisure and freedom for some, as well as heat, humidity and insects.

Take a moment to describe days in the season you are in now—either from the past or present. Do a cluster on one of your journal pages about images of this season, past and present. Put the name of the season in the center of the page. As you cluster, think about the following questions: Who is or was this season peopled with in your life? What activities repeat themselves this time of year? What buildings are there that you see? What goes on in the landscape? Are birds and animals coming or going? Do the markets have different fruits and vegetables, window dressings and products? Do the people around you wear different clothes and carry different things, including their expressions, than at other seasons?

Now that you have conjured your season, read these short excerpts from Thoreau's journals one early October:

> If they can't walk, why won't they take an honest nap and let me go in the afternoon? But, come two o'clock, they alarm me by an evident disposition to sit. In the midst of the most glorious Indian-summer afternoon, there they sit, breaking your chairs and wearing out the house, with their backs to the light, taking no note of the lapse of time.

and

> By the side of J.P. Brown's grain-field I picked up some white oak acorns in the path by the wood-side, which I found to be unexpectedly sweet and palatable, the bitterness being scarcely perceptible. . . . Such as these are no mean food. . . . Their sweetness is like the sweetness of bread, and to have discovered this palatableness in this neglected nut, the whole world is to me sweeter for it. . . . I should be at least equally pleased if I were to find that the grass tasted sweet and nutritious. It increases the number of my friends; it diminishes the number of my foes.

Where can you place yourself in your day and make a discovery from the season that thrills you? Where can you place yourself in your day that leads to happiness in a solitude away from those who do not share the excitement of the season?

You can begin your entry with these words: "It is _____ (early, middle, late) _____ (month of the year) and I am _____ (put an activity like walking, sitting, spying, sailing, chopping wood, cleaning gutters, calling the dogs in). It is _____ (insert an adjective that describes a feeling, e.g., lonely, crowded, pleasing, chilly, scary, comfortable). I am going to tell you why it is this way. . . ." From here on out you can roam around in the scene and in your thoughts from this season. Hopefully, you will make a discovery, sweet as Thoreau's acorn, during your roaming through this season's day, and the discovery that something or some persons in your day are crucial to who you are.

SIX EXTENSIONS OF THIS EXERCISE

1. Think of those people in Thoreau's entry breaking the chairs and wearing out the house with their sitting. Who in your life seems to slow you down or be unaware of all the excitement and beauty you find in the world around and inside you? Let them speak from that chair facing the wall where they can ignore the light. What are their thoughts?

2. Write in supplication to one of the people in your life who sits in those chairs, his or her back to the light. Write him out of his chair to visit the season with you.

3. Write about a day as if your writing were going into a time capsule to be unearthed in an epoch when the earth has changed geologically and the land and neighborhood where you are now will be gone. Preserve it in this season in your writing.

4. Write to a storekeeper or a crossing guard or a bird on a wire or a tree about to lose its leaves. Tell the person or thing how their presence and actions have mattered to you.

5. Plan a party to celebrate the season and write up the event. Who is invited and what do the invitations look like? Where is it held and what does the setting look like? What is served to the guests? What activities are planned for the party? What music? What do the pictures you took during the party look like?

6. How would Fall eulogize Summer or Summer eulogize Spring or Spring eulogize Winter or Winter eulogize Fall? Imagine the season you are in as the offspring of the season that came before it. Have it, as the only child, give a speech at its parent's memorial service. What does your season say on behalf of her mother or father? How does she praise and show affection and talk about what she has inherited?

WEEK SIX

The Interruption That Became an Inspiration

In her book, *Marry Your Muse: Making a Lasting Commitment to Your Creativity*, Jan Phillips writes about a day at a mountain cabin when she and her partner were spending time writing. Jan's cousins, ages ten and twelve, showed up at the door. When Jan told the girls that she and Annie were very busy writing, the girls said they understood, that they were writers, too. Jan invited the two girls in, saying they could all write for an hour till lunch, then eat and read their work to each other. When lunch was ready, the girls were still writing their stories and did not want to stop yet. When they did finish and eat lunch, all read their work to the others. Jan tells us how inspiring it was working alongside two girls who wrote because they hadn't forsaken the part of themselves that pulls out thoughts and tries them on "like clothes out of Grandma's closet."

This week, journal about the interruptions in your life so you can see how they might become inspirations. Start by clustering all the interruptions you've experienced recently. Choose one and write about it fully. Where were you and what were you hoping to or having to get done? What was the interruption? Capture it completely with dialogue and visual details: who, what, where, when, how. Tell the whole story. How did the interruption alter your work, day, plans, perceptions? What do you think about your redone day, plan, work or thoughts? What has the interruption inspired?

SIX EXTENSIONS OF THIS EXERCISE

One of the few things we can count on is being interrupted—by others, by noises, by news, by ourselves, by weather, accidents, illnesses, by decisions, dreams, vegetables burning on the stove and wind blowing the wires and the trees down.

1. Do another cluster about interruptions that have to do with nature and how it has impacted your life. Write on one of these times as you did previously.

2. Cluster about interruptions that are caused by things going wrong mechanically in your life. Choose one and write about it.

3. Cluster about interruptions to do with other people's decisions. Choose one and write about it.

4. Cluster about interruptions that have to do with your own thoughts and ideas. Choose a time this happened to you and write a vignette that shows what you were doing, then the thought that came along and what you did after the thought arrived.

5. Cluster about the people, pets, political and historical figures, or TV characters whose sudden deaths have interrupted your life. Choose one and write about it.

6. Cluster on dreams that have interrupted your life. This can be a night dream or a fantasy of what you would like things to be like. Choose one dream and describe it in detail. Tell what happened as a consequence of thinking about this dream or pursuing it. Write about how things changed for you, about the ways you were inspired to think differently or the reasons you delved into new areas or returned to old ones.

WEEK SEVEN
Grandma's Closet

I like the idea of trying on new thoughts like clothes out of a closet. Make that an attic, garage or basement full of stuff. Imagine yourself in such a storage area that belongs to you or to someone you know. Describe this place and then pull out one thing in particular. Describe it. Not only what it looks like, sounds like, feels like, smells like or tastes like, but what you think and remember when you look at and touch this object. If this object had to stand for one idea about your life or life in general, what would that be? Write about that in the form of an aphorism, proverb or just straightforward telling.

SIX EXTENSIONS OF THIS EXERCISE

1. Choose another item. This time let it speak and tell you what it remembers and thinks about life.

2. Choose something else and let it have a conversation with one or both of the things you already chose in the first two exercises this week. Make sure what they say really represents the point of view such an object would have in the world. If it has rust spots that make its arms sore, let's hear about it.

3. Choose another item and let it decide to walk away. Where is it going? Why is it leaving? What does it hope will happen or what does it hope to find? What does the world look like now after being tucked away for so long? Don't be afraid to be ridiculous—an old dish towel stained with motor oil can decide not to help make a fire and rather to roll and blow away as best it can relying on wind and people to transport it. There are many segments in a journey of trying to get from here to there.

4. Imagine a friend coming to visit you in the attic, garage or basement you have been envisioning all this week. Who is the friend? Why has she come? What do you want to show her amongst the stuff in that place? Tell your friend what you are showing her, then tell her why you are showing this item to her.

5. What does it smell like in this place you have been writing about all week in your journal? What causes the smell and what does it make you remember?

6. Imagine having a yard sale and getting rid of all the stuff in this storage place. Who is buying these things? Where are these things going? What do you have to say to them?

WEEK EIGHT
Finding the Tourist Within

In *The Writer's Journal: 40 Contemporary Writers and Their Journals*, Chitra Banerjee Divakaruni, poet and fiction writer, contributed notes from a journal entry in which she was writing about the difficulty of travel, "the helplessness of being lost and sweaty and constantly thirsty." In the same book, poet Naomi Shihab Nye writes that while traveling, "the abundance of sensory stimulation around us might make us expire. I wanted no more sounds or sights, no more flavors or fragrances."

It is not often that we think of touring as such hard work. But to the writer's sensitivity, it can be difficult because all of these sensations are calling out to be experienced and ultimately captured in words. How often we find our familiar daily world lacking in such sensory stimulation. It doesn't have to be that way. We can refresh ourselves about the experience of our daily world (whether it is more beautiful than we think or leaving us constantly sweaty and thirsty) by touring through it. For this journal entry, take a walk through a park, neighborhood, building, mall, house or even just a room that is familiar to you. Imagine you are visiting this place as if it were entirely new to you, and pretend you have an editor waiting for a travel article. What would you write to interest visitors and get them interested in visiting this location? What special hints would you give them about visiting your location?

SIX EXTENSIONS OF THIS EXERCISE

1. Write a letter from this place to someone who was once here with you. Point out what you are experiencing and let the person know whether you are glad or sad that they are not with you here.

2. Write a description of a packet of five postcards people can purchase at a gift store at this location. Write a message for each card you created, addressing each to a particular person in your life. Be sure to tell each addressee why you chose the particular image to send them.

3. Write a letter to someone who will never visit this place with you. Describe it so they will be sad not to have the opportunity.

4. Think of a flower, bird, song, poem or jingle that should be

adopted by this place. Write it down and then write about why this image fits the place so well.

5. Imagine you want to start a historical preservation society for this place. Write a proposal to the "powers that be" about why this place needs to be preserved.

6. Imagine that the place is being destroyed to make way for something new. You are the last visitor. Write about what will no longer be seen or experienced with its passing.

WEEK NINE
Finding the Motto Writer Within

We are motto happy in our culture. We circulate phrases from manufacturers and social service organizations from "Just Do It" to "Just Say No," from "You Deserve a Break Today" to "I Brake for Animals."

After I studied creative writing in graduate school and was publishing poetry, I started seriously working on longer writing. I was just starting to use a word processing program and my husband was customizing it to make it easier for me to use. He showed me the screen that came up when I booted up the word processing program. It had my name and then a blank line underneath that he said could say whatever I wanted (for many this was the place for the name of the company they worked for). I said, "Let it say, 'I'm a writer.'" That way, I thought, when the words came up, I would see my name followed by the affirmation that I am a writer and maybe I would get more writerly! At the same time that I was publishing my poetry and teaching writing and trying my hand at longer pieces, my mother seemed always to be saying, "Oh, you know who's a real writer?" She would supply the name of a distant cousin or friend's son who worked in television or advertising. When I got a new word processing program and my husband was again customizing it for me, he asked what I'd like that space to say this time. "I'm a real writer," I said without hesitation. The mottoes and tag lines we make for ourselves can get us going!

Imagine that today you are going to the personalized T-shirt store, bumper sticker store or the paint-your-own-mug-or-plate studio. You are going to make up a motto for yourself and put it on one of these objects. Start your journal entry by describing where you are when you get the idea to do this and what the motto says that you feel fits for you today. What will other people think or do when they see this motto? What do you hope to do as a result of having this motto be yours?

SIX EXTENSIONS OF THIS EXERCISE

1. Choose someone you love, like or respect and write a motto for them. Tell them in a letter why this is their motto and what you have made for them bearing this motto. What do you wish for them as a consequence of having this motto seen?

2. Choose someone who is bothering you and do the same exercise.

3. Write a letter to a parent explaining that now with hindsight you can articulate the motto you were raised with. Write it out and give examples of how your childhood rearing demonstrates the importance or dominance of this motto in your life.

4. Decide on a motto for your neighborhood, block, apartment building, office floor or social group. Write to one person in this group about your secret motto for the group. Tell the person you are writing to the reason you chose her to know your secret motto.

5. Write a motto that is a direct opposite of the motto you wrote

for yourself at the beginning of the week. Write a dialogue between two parts of yourself—one of which lives by the first motto and one of which lives by the second one. Put your two selves in a particular situation or action, e.g., buying a car, deciding on a vacation, signing up for a new exercise class. Let them talk about the situation with a perspective based on their individual mottoes.

6. Write a new motto for the whole country. For instance, President John F. Kennedy was famous for his words, "Ask not what your country can do for you—ask what you can do for your country." Imagine yourself being inaugurated into a powerful position and giving a speech. You can draw from personal experience when you write the motto and tell why you have come to know how important it is to live by.

WEEK TEN
Metaphor for My Life Right Now

This morning I had breakfast with Sam Turner, a man who lost his twenty-three-year-old son less than two years ago. He was telling me that because he has to appear the strong male, his grieving process continues in isolated moments when he is alone. He said he'll be driving and his eyes will fill up with so many tears that he'll have to pull off to the side of the road until the sudden wave of sadness dissipates. He likes to write and is a good writer, so I imagined a whole book for him, a collection of personal essays called, "Pulling Off to the Side of the Road." It seems that the work of grieving must be done off the road and at odd and unexpected moments. Pulling off the road seems like a good metaphor for the emotional work and state he finds himself in.

With what are you concerned emotionally or spiritually or in your work or family life? Write about this. Put in very specific details about where you are when you deal with the concern. My friend, for instance, could tell what highways or roads he drives on alone, what thoughts or images or memories enter his head that make his eyes tear up. He can write about how long he stays pulled over, what he does to dry his tears and when it is he knows he can resume driving. After you are done writing, see if you can find a metaphor in the writing itself that evokes the state of being you have been describing. Use it as a title to this entry.

SIX EXTENSIONS OF THIS EXERCISE

1. Write about a place you have visited as a consequence of the concern you wrote about. Describe it fully even if it is not unusual or, on the surface of things, not an interesting place.

2. Write about something you have purchased during the time you have been in the state you have written about. My friend, who is not Jewish, purchased a menorah because a woman in his support group told them all how much her young son had loved the holiday of Hanukkah. He and his wife started lighting the candles and with each night of the eight dedicated their lighting to a friend or family member they wanted to think about.

3. Write about a person who is connected to you in this time of spiritual, emotional or work concern. Describe this person physically. Let this person talk in your writing. What is she saying?

4. Write about a decision or resolution you have made as a direct outcome of the situation you have been writing about. What happened once you made this decision?

5. Write a letter to someone close to you telling them why you would not have had this time in your life be any different

than it is. This will be hard if it is a difficult time you are
describing. You may experience wanting it to be different
than it is. However, if you write "as if" you wouldn't change
it, you will honor this time, and you will discover great
strength.

6. Describe an object in your life that you could decide to give
    away during the time you are writing about. To whom might
    you give it and why? Be detailed about the object and the
    recipient and the reasons for giving.

WEEK ELEVEN
The Words They Taught Me

I have a collection of words given to me by other people: *hegemony*,
and *prehensile* are words a lover taught me years ago. He was a
professor, and he'd stop in conversation and explain the meanings
of words I didn't know. Some of the words he taught me fit him,
I thought. He liked total control over things and he seemed to
grab at a woman's desire to be helpful to him. When I was done
seeing him, I took his words with me. For instance, I had an
experimental cardboard piece of artwork on my dining room wall
for years. It had wings that stood out from the wall and people
passing by on their way to a chair often brushed past and were
hooked. Prehensile art, I thought to myself each time that happened. Art should grab at you, shouldn't it? *Hegemony* I applied
to myself, finally. I'd made it difficult for my second husband to
cook in our (read that "my") kitchen. I didn't want to lose hegemony over it. I didn't want to lose hegemony over a lot of things
after six years between marriages.

Presentable was an early word I received. My father used to dress
each morning in his suit and tie ready to meet the doctors and
nurses to whom he was going to sell pharmaceuticals (that's another

word I got from him along with *laboratory*—and I was only six!). *Indispensable* is one, too. He used to say, "In business, no one is indispensable." He felt he had to remember that every working day of his life so he would work hard and never feel complacent. The words I learned from my father were very costly words. His words were from a world view of competition, striving for acceptance and persistent insecurity covered by dark suits and tasteful ties and lightly starched white shirts, the color of the ever present paperwork inside his black and white Chevy sedans.

Write a list of at least seven words other people taught you. Choose one of the words and describe the person who taught it to you, where you were when you learned it and how you use it today.

SIX EXTENSIONS OF THIS EXERCISE

1. Choose another word from the list you made. Write about the person who taught you the word, where you were when you learned the word and how you use the word today.
2. Do this for another word on the list.
3. And another.
4. And another.
5. And another.
6. And one more.

WEEK TWELVE
Return to Morrie's Window

It has been ten weeks since you did the exercise about adopting a window or a place to write about. For your journal entry this week, go back to your adopted window or outdoor place and sit awhile. Once again, jot down what you see, hear, feel, smell and even taste because you are sitting in this spot now. Things have changed, you have changed. Your impressions and memories will change.

Again, imagine yourself director of your own short film about your adopted place. What does the camera select today for the viewer to see—people and their activities, plants, animals, man-made technologies and buildings?

What small things will the camera zoom in on? Where will the camera pan? Who walks on screen? What ambient sounds are on the soundtrack?

Now that the scene is evoked, let someone or something suddenly fill up or darken the camera's lens. Anyone or anything that pops into your mind can pop into this scene. People and pets and objects are sometimes where we recognize the eternal and our connection to it.

In your writing become the voice-over in a documentary. Ask this figure why he or she has come. Record the answer. For example, "When I asked my seventh grade math teacher why she was walking outside my window today, she looked toward the bricks on the house across the street and asked me to name the geometric shapes in the outer walls. I said the words. . . ."

SIX EXTENSIONS OF THIS EXERCISE

1. Go to the same window or place and see who or what pops up to talk to you. If it is the same person or thing, write more of what is told.

2. Pretend you are enlarging one part of the scene. Describe what you are enlarging. What do you see now that the object or person is bigger? Write for ten minutes on what is revealed with the enlargement. You can begin, "Until I magnified what I was looking at, I didn't. . . ."

3. This time imagine a deaf person in the scene you have written about. Write the scene from her point of view.

4. Again, do the list of lines about the scene in your adopted place where each line starts with the words, "Because I know my time is almost done." Continue each line with something you observe through the senses, e.g., "Because I know my time is almost done, I don't mind the tent caterpillar on the top branch of the pine tree, the bounty of needles there to feed its larvae." "Because I know my time is almost done, I want to eat the peaches from my neighbor's tree now, though they don't ripen for months." Now it's your turn: "Because I know my time is almost done, I. . . ."

5. Write about something that you wish could stay untouched in this spot. Why do you wish this?

6. Time alters everything, though. Imagine the something you wished could stay the same changing over time. Describe the changes.

WEEK THIRTEEN
Self-Reflection Week

In the work world there are quarterly reviews in which employees do self-evaluations on how well they have done their jobs. Bosses also evaluate each employee's progress. Here is your opportunity as both hirer of the journal keeper and as journal keeper to write a progress report.

First write from the boss' point of view. How well did the employee fulfill the job description? What were the journal keeper's successes these past twelve weeks? In what way, if any, did the journal keeper disappoint you? You may want to read through the twelve weeks of entries to refresh your memory.

Now, switch your point of view and write the journal keeper's self-evaluation. In what ways was the job satisfying? In what ways was the job disappointing? Is there anything you need from the boss to be able to better do your job? Explain what these things are and how they might be provided.

SIX EXTENSIONS FOR SELF-REFLECTION

1. Choose a journal entry. Read back through it, noting places where you could have included more detail. For instance, you may have used the word *nice* or the word *beautiful* when you actually had the opportunity to show what made you judge a person, situation or thing as nice or beautiful. A nice postman may be one who recognizes you and greets you by name or always delivers mail even if there is postage due because he trusts that you'll leave the money for him the next day. A beautiful child might be one whose hair is as curly as an artisan's wood shavings. Circle the words that generalize where detail could have evoked more of the experience you had. Make arrows from each circle to a space on the page where you can write a few details.

After awhile you will learn that when you are writing entries, if you feel stuck or bored with what you are saying, you can choose one of the five senses and challenge yourself to write a detail about what you experienced directly through your eyes, ears, nose, tongue or skin. Writers call this "staying in the scene" and "showing instead of telling." Emphasizing the use of sensory detail is useful to the journal writer because it allows her to write without prejudging what she is saying. The showing without telling will ultimately help the journal writer write longer, fuller entries that offer fresh insight.

2. Look through this quarter's worth of your journal entries. Underline five nouns you seem to use more than you knew you did. How many times did you use each of those five nouns? If you had to make those five words fit into a category, what would the category be? Now try to figure out more than one category the words could fit into. The categories might not be mutually exclusive. For instance, one poet uses the words *stone*, *earth*, *river*, *sky* and *heron* frequently. We could say those words fit into the category of "outdoors" but they also fit into the categories "not being possessed by any one group," "above and below," "still and moving," "vast and small," "without words but with music." Make as many categories as you can into which your five words fit.

Now make five statements about what it means to you that you can see these categories in your writing. For instance, for the poet we were just talking about, the statements might be: (1) I hear the music of the earth in what belongs to us all. (2) If I didn't notice what is still, I would not know about what moves. (3) If I didn't see what moves, I might forget that so much is still. (4) So much is bigger than me and will outlast me; therefore I look at it all through the eyes of one (the heron) who can get above. (5) When I observe the word-less in my world, I recognize more than I can when I listen only to words.

Next write questions about your use of these words. Examples might be: (1) When I use each of these five words in my entries, what feeling am I experiencing? (2) What memories do I have of noticing stones? (3) When I think of a river, which one am I really picturing? (4) When in my life now do I look at the sky or the earth? (5) When was the last time I saw a heron? The first time?

By thinking about words you see in your entries as a kind of emotional shorthand, you might experience the themes you are exploring more deeply in your heart and body.

3. After you have written the five statements and five questions, do freewrites in your journal attempting to answer the questions. Choose one of your questions and spend twenty minutes writing an answer that satisfies you.

4. Choose one more of the questions and do a freewrite attempting to answer the question.

5. Work with a third question doing a freewrite to answer it.

6. And one more time, write freely for twenty minutes answering one of your two remaining questions.

ෆ

At the exercise class where I work out on a stationary bicycle in a room full of fellow "bicyclists," we "follow" our leader up an imagined hill and onto the open road, where we "pass" other cyclists and work our way up another hill before we get to the next open road. At the ride's end, we raise our arms over our heads, and we clap at the success of our ride. Although we each go at our own speed and adjust the bikes to our own levels of resistance, we all start together and we all finish together. We all get a good workout.

Find a picture of someone exercising that you think captures your sense of keeping a journal. Paste it onto the last page of your first quarter's work. Congratulations on finishing your first quarter's journey!

Take a deep breath. Bring your arms up over the top of your head. Exhale, bringing them down. You know your own heart rate better than before. Onward to the next quarter!

CHAPTER SIX

Second Quarter

The play of shine and shade on the trees as the supple
boughs wag,
The delight alone or in the rush of the streets, or along the
fields and hillsides,
The feeling of health . . . the full-noon trill . . . the song
of me rising from bed and meeting the sun.

WALT WHITMAN
Leaves of Grass

Continuing a commitment or project takes a different kind of energy than making fresh starts. It is in the continuing that we realize the excitement of the honeymoon with our new journal is over. Our partner, the journal, is not new and unknown anymore. Some of the mystery and anticipation is being replaced with the sameness of keeping our ritual going. We may feel cranky and find rebellious feelings creeping in if we feel harnessed to this work.

This is a good time to be inspired by the poet Walt Whitman and the way he thought of himself in *Leaves of Grass*. If we persist in our desire to observe, we re-energize ourselves.

A Walker in the City, Town or Village

Alfred Kazin, author of *A Walker in the City*, writes in his contribution to the book *Inventing the Truth: The Art and Craft of Memoir:*

I was trying to write something about the city at large that would do justice to the color, the variety, the imperial range I encountered walking about the city every day. Every next day I tried to get into my notebook what Whitman in his greatest New York poem, "Crossing Brooklyn Ferry," had called "the glories strung like beads on my smallest sights and hearings— on the walk in the street, and the passage over the river."

Now it is your turn to take inspiration from Whitman. Illustrate the lines I chose for the epigraph at the start of this chapter the way Kazin speaks of illustrating the "glories strung like beads." Describe a tree you see each day, a street you drive or walk upon, a field or hillside near your home. Describe yourself rising from bed to meet the sun there.

SIX EXTENSIONS OF THIS EXERCISE

1. Another New York poet, Frank O'Hara, wrote a poem in which the sun talks to him and urges him out of bed. Write a conversation between you and the sun. What has the sun come to tell you and how do you answer? What do you think about after the conversation?

2. Try this with the moon. Describe yourself rising from bed to meet the moon and write the conversation you have.

3. Try this with the fresh air you will encounter when you open your door in the morning. What does the air have to say to you and you to it?

4. Go into a supermarket today and walk slowly up and down each aisle imagining yourself seeing this store and its contents for the first time. Write a letter about the store and what you marvel at to someone who can't be there with you.

5. Think of a small area you know well but usually don't think about—a hall closet, an empty lot, the garage where you park your car. Write three paragraphs of praise for this place and the particulars about it. Don't worry if it seems silly and far-fetched. Just let yourself find details to praise.

6. Imagine an untaken photograph of yourself in a place you know well. Describe this photograph and how you came to be there and who would have taken the picture.

WEEK FIFTEEN
Soul Between the Lines

In her book *Soul Between the Lines: Freeing Your Creative Spirit Through Writing*, Dorothy Randall Gray talks about a method she calls finding seeds. She says those words that have an extra charge for us are important, whether they are our own words and phrases or those of others we overhear. This week write a journal entry about a sentence you overheard recently or in the past and what you made of the words. The words might have floated by or seemed to thrust toward you like a sword. Begin your writing by telling where were you when you heard the words. Who was saying them? How did they stay with you the rest of your day? How do you feel and what do you think of as you write them down now?

SIX EXTENSIONS OF THIS EXERCISE

1. Let your finger fall at random onto five words in printed material around you. List these words. Now write one journal entry that incorporates all the words.

2. Ask a friend to give you five words. Write a horoscope for this friend that uses all the words.

3. Think of five names you've been called or phrases people

always seem to apply to you. Write about whether they fit you or not. "You called me _____," you might write before continuing, "and/but actually. . . ."

4. Look at a bookshelf full of books. Grab five words from different titles. Make these words into a title, adding more words if necessary. Don't worry if you make up a long title. Now write a small story inspired by this title.

5. If you were going to set sail on a boat built just for you, what would you name the boat? Write about what the name means and why you have used it.

6. Imagine you are in a room full of people who you will be working with all day. The group leader asks you all to list seven things someone might be interested in knowing about you. List them. Next, imagine the leader asks you to introduce yourself to the group by talking about those things. Write down what you would be saying to the group.

WEEK SIXTEEN
Affirm, Affirm, Affirm

Once a colleague at a university gave me an intriguing gift she had made. It was a plastic jar full of strips of paper—pastel blue, canary, pale green and white. Each piece of paper had an affirmation typed onto it. Mary said to pluck out a strip of paper each day and it would tell me something I needed to know that day. For your journal entry this week, you will design an affirmation kit for yourself. You must start by writing down at least seven affirmations. Affirmations are statements that clarify and give permission to think in a positive way. "I am at peace and the world brings peace to me," is an example of an affirmation. Here are two more: "I see the happiness around me and I rejoice in it." "I compliment people for their good deeds and rich perception." After you have written the affirmations, choose one and write about areas of your life that would benefit from you using this affirmation. Describe things as they are and write about how the affirmation would help you concentrate on something important.

SIX EXTENSIONS OF THIS EXERCISE
---

1. Choose another affirmation and write the same kind of meditation.
2. Choose another and do the same.
3. Choose another and do the same.
4. Choose another and do the same.
5. Choose another and do the same.
6. Choose one more and do the same.

WEEK SEVENTEEN
Confetti

Write down six secrets you are keeping at this time—they can be a combination of big and small, good and bad. Maybe they are something like this: "I had to go to the bathroom while I was on the phone with an important client, but I couldn't think of an appropriate way to say I'd call him back." "I bought a $100 birthday present for my mother that cost more than the gift allowance my husband and I have decided on." "I think I'm pregnant." "I am not telling my friends that the way they criticize food keeps me from enjoying my food when we go out to eat." "I broke my diet again but won't tell my husband, who has been dieting with me." "I don't really want to hike up the canyon even though I said I would." "I'm seeing a therapist." Write about each secret. Why is it a secret? Who is it a secret from? What do you fear would happen if you told that person the secret?

SIX EXTENSIONS OF THIS EXERCISE

1. Choose six words, one from each secret. Mine might be: *bathroom*, *$100*, *criticize*, *diet*, *hike*, *therapist*. Imagine you have torn up your list of secrets and thrown the paper to the wind. Write about where one of these words has landed. Is it now under the feet of a mink-coated woman walking her dog on a fancy downtown street? What does she make of this message from the skies? Is the word lying on a tulip blossoming in the fields? What does the word imply lying there on the flower?

2. "Word spread all over town"—this is what we say about news that's gotten out. Imagine one of your secrets spreading all over town—in headlines, news reports, talk show hosts' conversations, billboards. Write the story of the day that the news spread all over town.

3. Think about one of the secrets you wrote about in extension number one. What would it be like if you didn't have this secret? You might surprise yourself with how many things important to you exist because of what is in your secret.

4. Are you holding a secret for someone else? Choose a word from this secret and cast it to the wind. Where does this word end up? Describe where it has landed and write about what goes on around it.

5. Think about more secrets you are holding for others. Imagine weighing one of them (whether you write it down or not). There are many kinds of scales—the kind trucks use on interstate freeways, your bathroom or gym scale, the scale at the produce or meat and fish section of a market, a postal scale, the scale at your doctor's office. What was it like bringing this secret to the scale you chose? How heavy was this secret?

Was that a surprise? What will you do with the secret now that you know how much it weighs?

6. Think about a secret wish of yours to be or to have something. Imagine writing down this secret and tearing up the paper you wrote it on. Write what your thoughts would be as you ripped each word of the secret apart from the other words. What would you think as you cast each word to the wind?

WEEK EIGHTEEN
Chasing the Caribou

Ian Frazier writes in his contribution to *Inventing the Truth: The Art and Craft of Memoir*, "I've seen films of wolves pursuing a herd of caribou. They will pick one out. The wolf will run into a herd of thousands and will chase that one caribou through the herd—and get it." He says "When you are in a field and whole bunch of quail go up, if you're a beginner you put your gun to your shoulder and just go BANG. You see all those birds and you shoot at them all and you won't get one. If you want to get a bird, pick *one* bird and shoot it." Frazier says these hunting analogies are useful to the writer. Get one thing right, he advises.

A detail or observation that seems right to you can be the basis for something much larger. This week, your journaling will provide an opportunity to get that one thing right (and written). Take a moment to cluster about events in your life. They can range from weddings and funerals to business conferences and birthday parties or TGIFs with colleagues. Choose one of these events and cluster about the memories you have from it. Who was there? Why were you there? Where did it take place? Be detailed and specific. Reconstruct the event so it can be re-experienced. Then write about something valuable you learned during this event or just after. How do you know you learned it?

SIX EXTENSIONS OF THIS EXERCISE

---

1. Think about your day. What is one detail or observation that means a lot to you—maybe more to you than to anyone else. Write it down and write about how you came to see, hear, taste, touch or smell what it is you are writing about.

2. Look around the room you are in now. What is your favorite of all the things you looked at? Describe it and tell why it is special in this moment.

3. Look around the room you are in now. What is your favorite of all the things you could touch? Describe how it feels and tell why it is special in this moment.

4. Look around the room you are in now. What is your favorite of all the things you could smell? Write about this smell. Why is it important to you?

5. Listen in the room you are in now. What is your favorite sound? Or think about sounds the objects in the room could make. What would be your favorite? Describe it. Compare it to other sounds. Why is this sound special? What does it make you think about or do?

6. Look around the room you are in now. What would have a taste you'd find interesting if you were to put this thing in your mouth? What would it make you remember or think?

WEEK NINETEEN
Before and After

When I was a girl I read my mother's women's magazines cover to cover—*Good Housekeeping, Family Circle* and *Woman's Day*.

What really hooked me were the before and after pictures and stories—house remodels; makeup, wardrobe and hairdo makeovers; pictures of clients involved in weight loss programs, stories of bad marriages turned good after counseling. The whole world started looking like before and after—the way to school in the morning and the way home after you'd been in school all day, your teeth with braces and your teeth after the braces were taken off, the puppy adopted from the pound the day you brought her home and the puppy weeks after she was a member of the family, watching TV before dinner and watching it after you did your homework. Write a "before and after" that occurs to you, adding in details about what you are remembering. For instance:

My idea of a college wardrobe before I left for college was mix and match sweaters, skirts and slacks as seen in *Seventeen* and *Vogue*. My idea of a college wardrobe after I was at school a couple of months was blue jeans and sweatshirts. It was so hard to spend time on getting dressed and keeping clothes looking good when I had papers to write and ten books to read each week. Jeans never meant as much to me as they did at the University of Wisconsin. Especially in winter—long johns underneath, wool socks, Clark's desert boots, a warm coat, hat and gloves. I would make it to class and peel the layers off in the warmly heated buildings. We all began to look the same that year. I know at least one young man in one of my classes felt ripped off by the nature of our wardrobes. He was not an attractive person, but he felt righteous enough to say something about how all the women were certainly letting themselves go. . . .

Continue writing your memory!

SIX EXTENSIONS OF THIS EXERCISE

Write a long list of before and afters filling at least one page. For each additional day you want to write this week, choose one of these and write about it. Or make up a new before and after each day that you sit down to write. Describe the before part in detail. Then switch to the after part and describe it in detail.

WEEK TWENTY
I Know How to Do This

Even though we want to come to journaling with the idea that we are "not knowing" about our writing, we still can use the writing time to recount the things we know how to do. One way to combine the telling with the not knowing is to think of a person to whom you want to explain how to do something or how something is made. You probably won't fully know why you are telling the person what you are telling them until you are well into the writing.

Take some time to cluster on what you know how to do or make. Cluster also on people you might address on the various topics. Choose one subject and the person you are going to write to. Write this person a letter about making or doing this thing. After you have described the process, explain to the person why you are telling her about it.

For example, Tim Johnson, one of my students, decided he would write about how pinto beans are cultivated and harvested. Tim had land in North Dakota he was leasing to his cousin who was going to raise the crop and bring it to market. He realized he wanted to tell the process to a friend and colleague, and in the course of writing he figured out why—the farming analogies applied to his friend's journey of the last eight years healing from the murder of his wife, the tracking down of the assailant and ultimately the ability to remarry and continue with his life. Tim writes with many analogies between the growing of the beans and the friend's life. Here is a small sample:

> I am willing to risk guaranteed cash rent for a share of the pinto bean crop. In part, I am willing to assume the risk for the long-term benefit of soil stewardship. You more than anyone know that life doesn't come with guarantees and without risk. Eight years ago 100 percent of your life was at risk. Slowly but surely you have been able to turn the situation around from that of an operator who assumes all the risks to that of a landlord, like me, who is still willing to risk 20 percent in order to be a better steward.

SIX EXTENSIONS OF THIS EXERCISE

1. Think of something else you know how to do and someone you'd like to tell this information to. As you write, keep in mind the person you think you are writing it to until you can write down the reason you are telling the information to her.

2. Choose another process and another person to write to. The processes you describe this week can be as daily as how to get out of the house in the morning in under a half hour or as important as how to mend a marriage. Vary the "importance" of the processes you write about over this week as well as the person you have selected for an audience.

3. Choose another process to write about and person to write to about it.

4. And another.

5. And another.

6. And another.

There Ought to Be a Word for This

Do you ever notice something that seems to go on or happen over and over again and there is no one word for it? Different languages have words for different human interactions or events in the natural world. For instance, the Scotch have a name for the kind of person who always shows up around dinnertime. It is not merely a word that means "mooch." It is specific to the action of showing up around dinnertime when the person will have to be invited to stay.

Think about behaviors you have that you really don't like in yourself. Describe yourself doing these behaviors. As you describe them, give each one a name. You can borrow words from another language or a special lingo, or you can make up words or string words together with hyphens to create a term that aptly describes this behavior.

SIX EXTENSIONS OF THIS EXERCISE

1. Take one of the behaviors you described and create a support group for people who suffer from this behavior. Write a description of one meeting of the group.

2. Take one of the behaviors you described and imagine a support group for people who have to live with people with that behavior. Write a description of one meeting of that group.

3. Imagine yourself going on TV as an expert in the field of study of one of these behaviors. What questions are you asked by an interviewer and what are your answers?

4. Imagine a treatment created for one of these behaviors. Describe it and how one takes this treatment.

5. Imagine one of the behaviors as incurable. How does it progress?

6. Imagine one of these behaviors is genetic. What symptoms do you find in future generations?

If I Were a Rich Man

These days there are a lot of people coming into unexpected wealth—lottery winners, people lucky in the stock market, software company employees, doctors bought out of managed care partnerships by insurance companies. It all makes me think of the musical I saw on Broadway as a young adult, *Fiddler on the Roof*. While the main character, a poor farmer, plays his violin atop a house, he ruminates about what he'd do if he were a rich man. One thing he'd do is "deedle, deedle, dee." This makes me think it is indeed hard for a laborer to imagine what a rich person might do all day.

Write a description of where you are while you think about being rich—very, very rich. Are you on a rooftop or in a stairwell, at an intersection or parking meter? Write "If I were a rich person, I'd . . . ," using some of the imagery from where you are as you think about being rich. The more detailed you can be, the more you will realize that some of this wealth is already in your life.

SIX EXTENSIONS OF THIS EXERCISE

Imagine other fates that could befall you and write about those. Here are six ideas, but you may come up with many of your own:

1. If I were a starving person
2. If I were a smoker (or a nonsmoker)
3. If I were a world leader
4. If I had a great voice (or tennis swing, swimming stroke, way with color, etc.)

5. If I weren't married (or were married)
6. If I were a teenager (or a member of any age bracket not currently yours)

Each day take a turn and write an "If I," including details of the place from which you imagine this situation.

This Is a Story About

When my daughter was graduating from college, she received an honor that required she present a speech before thousands of people. When she heard about the requirement, she was also working hard to finish the last of her course work. She scarcely had time to write the speech that was very important to her. I suggested she adapt a writing exercise I use with students that helps them gather information and images about their topics. Her topic was her experience at the college these past four years; how that would all fall together into a speech with meaning and a little entertainment value was the unknown part. I told her to write a long list of everything she could remember about her time at college by starting every line with "This is a speech about. . . ." She did this, and it wasn't long before she was in touch with her experience and very able to find a structure for its presentation. She invented a walk around campus noting what she saw and remembered from her years at college, stating that her speech could be about all of these. For example, she wrote:

My speech could be about the old stacks at Doe, the dusty books one hundred years old, the nine-story tall bookshelves, the glass tile floor at the ninth tier, about looking down through glass at centuries of knowledge. It could be about visiting the particle accelerator on the hill, about my professor's ultra-low temperature physics lab, about a Styrofoam cup of liquid nitrogen, and finding leaves and twigs to freeze. It could be about walking each day past parking spaces reserved for Nobel Laureates, about sitting in on a contemporary American poetry course taught by new United States Poet Laureate Professor Robert Hass. My speech could be about coming to Cal because I knew it was a great university but realizing I didn't know at the time what great university meant. . . .

Think of a situation you want to describe—a place you studied, worked or visited, or an era in your life. Create a piece of writing about it with the lines, "This is a story about. . . ." Repeat this line or a version of it as often as you need to keep finding more to say.

SIX EXTENSIONS OF THIS EXERCISE

1. Think of a person you want to describe. Make the list of lines starting with "This is a story about. . . ."

2. Think of your day. Write a list that has lines starting with "This was a day about . . . ."

3. Think of a conversation you had recently or want to have. Write about it using lines that repeat "This was/is a conversation about . . ."

4. Think about a drive you take regularly. Write about it using lines that begin, "This is a drive about. . ."

5. Think about a walk or a run you take regularly and write about it using lines that repeat, "This is a walk about. . . ."

6. Think about a holiday you enjoy or don't enjoy or have mixed

feelings about. Write about that using lines that start, "This is a story about. . . ."

Things to Do

While we are using lists, here's another week's entry that allows us to write and describe while depending on a list. Poet Gary Snyder wrote "Things to Do Around a Lookout" from his experience as a fire lookout in the California forests. He includes things in his list like airing out musty forest service sleeping bags, drinking Lapsang souchong tea, reading old *Reader's Digest* magazines and the *Star Book.* He talks about bathing in snow melt on a warm day.

This week your opportunity is to think about unusual places you inhabit or have inhabited that you don't usually write about. They can be real places, like a dentist's chair, a piano bench shared with a piano teacher, the driver's seat in a traffic jam, a bus stop or the fiction aisles at your favorite bookstore. They can be imaginary like inside a crocus blossom or a spider's web. Start this entry by calling it "Things to Do While _____ (plug in name of this place)." See how many specific things you can imagine yourself doing in this location. For instance, if you are in a dentist's chair you can fiddle with the headphone radio stations until you find some hard rock to drown out the sound of the dentist's tools cracking around inside your mouth. You can leaf through the six-month-old *People Magazine* the hygienist brought to you and read about a celebrity's wedding knowing she has already left her husband. You can think about the grocery list in the front seat of your car with items neatly written down—milk, eggs, butter, asparagus, brie. You can stare at the turtle-shaped pin on the assistant's pastel blue uniform, or you can think about how you forgot to leave food out for the cats. You can. . . . The listing will take on a momentum of its own and become a satisfying way of describing experience. For this to happen, write in full sentences.

SIX EXTENSIONS OF THIS EXERCISE

1. Choose a different strange location to write about in this listy way for every day you want to write this week.

2. Use occasions rather than places: "Things to Do While Waiting for My Husband to Get Ready to Go Out With Me" or "Things to Do While I'm Seething With Rage at My Teenage Child."

3. You can revisit uncomfortable times from the past by calling entries something like "Things to Do While Mrs. Boor Is Marking Up My Latest Assignment in Second Grade" or "Things to Do While My Mother and Father Quarrel and Slam Doors" or "Things to Do the Moment Your Soon-to-Be Ex Leaves After Telling You He's Found Someone Else."

4. You can plan ahead using this entry style for future events and responsibilities: "Things to Do When Planning a Wedding," "Things to Do When Entering Therapy," "Things to Do When Getting a Promotion," "Things to Do When Getting Laid Off." Let the lines in your list range from the small and seemingly unimportant (e.g., linger over three cups of coffee in your bathrobe) to the more important (e.g. take out the phone book and locate the nearest unemployment office). Every detail of your experience is important and helps tell your experience.

5. You can evoke your own strengths in the midst of sadness or fear with entries titled something like "Things to Do When You Want a Happy Ending to a Breakup" or "Things to Do When You Never Want to Suffer Stage Fright Again." You

can write on "Things to Do When You're Afraid to Talk About _____ (sex, money, loneliness, commitment, etc.)."

6. "Things to Do When You Want to Remember a Loved One No Longer Alive" is a good list to help you conjure up someone you don't want to forget.

WEEK TWENTY-FIVE
Burying the Dutch Oven

One of my writing colleagues shared in an essay that when she angrily broke up with a beloved college boyfriend under duress because her father didn't like him, she took the Dutch oven they used for cooking and buried it in the backyard before she left. The topic of the essay was finding him fifteen years later and marrying him, metaphorically unearthing the pot. Burying the past and unburying are both about letting go. By writing about tangible objects we can both do and undo.

Cluster a list of things in your house that were given to you by other people. Choose one of these items; it can be one you like or dislike. For whatever reason, even if you don't want to, imagine you are going to give it a burial somewhere specific today. Write about the object, how it came to be in your house, why it is time to bury it and where you will bury it. Describe yourself digging a hole. How do you carry it to the place you will bury it? What do you say as you bury the object? What do you think when you arrive back in your house again?

SIX EXTENSIONS OF THIS EXERCISE

1. Think of an object in your home that you overlook, an object that can hold things on or in it—e.g., bulletin board, stainless mixing bowl, mailbox, recycling container, bedroom trash

can. Write about this object in adoring phrases especially noting its functional qualities. Now that you have spoken about how this object functions, write about a discomfort in your life by imagining yourself putting the discomfort on or into the ever present object.

2. Imagine and write about a special bowl that you would design to put somewhere in your home. It is going to be a bowl into which you can put what you don't want to think about. You can drop messages about those things into the bowl. After you have fully described the bowl, you might want to give it a name. Next, write one of the messages about what you no longer want to think about. Be detailed and specific. Cover everything regarding whatever it is you are going to give up thinking about. Write about dropping that message in the bowl.

3. Write another message for the bowl. Write about dropping it into the bowl.

4. And again.

5. And again.

6. And again.

Self-Reflection Week

The ending of the second quarter represents six months of employment. What do you have to say about the job the journal keeper has done this second three months? Look back at last quarter's evaluation and remind yourself what the boss and the hire each wrote that required attention. Have the needs been addressed and met this quarter? Are there new needs now and new methods to meet them? You can write about all of this in a letter from the boss to the journal keeper and a letter back from the journal keeper to the boss.

SIX EXTENSIONS FOR SELF-REFLECTION

1. William Zinsser edited a book in 1988 called *Spiritual Quests: The Art and Craft of Religious Writing.* In his introduction to the book, Zinsser states that "the act of writing is ultimately a sacrament for both writer and reader." The act of writing sustains the writer in his or her quest. In writing, spiritual energy seems to flow in at times and alter our perception. It almost directs the writing. This spiritual energy feels sometimes like a loss of control, but it is really an important renunciation of a certain part of the mind, Zinsser writes. That is the part of the mind that wants to control thoughts. Only when we let go of thoughts can we be free to listen to a deeper voice within. Look over your entries this quarter. Where do you note a deeper voice popping up and dispelling the preconceived thoughts with which you may have started writing some of the entries? Write in your journal about as many of these entries as you can. Write about how you see the difference between the preconceived ideas you brought to the writing and the ones that arrived as you were writing.

2. List five words or phrases in the sentences that you feel are holding preconceived thoughts. Write about associations you have with these words. Where do you imagine you are when you hear or read each of them? In a classroom? At a travel lecture? At the motor vehicles licensing place? You might write, "When I read words in sentences in which I have included preconceived thoughts my voice sounds like a gavel hitting the judge's bench." Continue describing the sound of

these words to fully hear the difference between being dull and off the point, and being vibrant and true.

3. List five words or phrases you use in the sentences that you feel are full of unexpected energy. Where do you imagine you could be when you hear or read each of these words? An example might be, "When I read words in sentences I have written in which a new energy arrives, my voice carries me like sails full of wind." Continue these descriptions to more fully evoke an understanding of your voices, both dull and vibrant.

4. Take some of the sentences that carry preconceived ideas and rewrite them. Scramble the words in a new order, or pick and choose words from several of these sentences until you have as many new sentences as you have ones that carry preconceived ideas. Write a poem whose first stanza is a list of the sentences from your journal and whose second stanza is a list of the new sentences. What do you feel in this juxtaposition?

5. Take one of the sentences that has preconceived ideas in it and put it in the mouth of a disliked teacher. Now write a note to a classmate (like the ones we used to pass around among our desks) on which you say why you dislike this teacher and what she is saying.

6. Take one of the sentences that has ideas and words with welcome energy. Imagine it is being spoken by a substitute teacher who has come in for the day to take that disliked teacher's place. Write another note to pass about the way you respond to this teacher and what he is saying.

∞

You have traveled through another quarter of your year's journey. You've seen some new sights, revisited familiar ones and stopped

101

along the way to take in whatever was there. Yes, there were a lot of miles covered. Yes, it was a trip of a lifetime!

Paste a travel picture onto the last page of your second quarter, one you think captures something of yourself on this part of your journey.

All aboard for the third quarter!

CHAPTER SEVEN

Third Quarter

And now I sit here weary at my computer. Willow-Cat is sleeping on my desk nearby. Somewhere in another room, Springsteen is singing, "I'm on Fire." And somewhere, out there, the sun is on fire. Somewhere beyond my bedroom window and the garden wall, beyond the oleander bushes and the asphalt-shingled roofs and the TV antennas, beyond the drone of the evening news and the roar of the rush-hour traffic, the sun blazes silently above the blue Estrella Mountains. . . .

G. LYNN NELSON
Writing and Being: Taking Back Our Lives
Through the Power of Language

You are now halfway through a year of journaling. Perhaps it is getting harder to push away the world that rushes around with you caught in its current. But, hopefully, it is getting easier and easier to find those sandbars of time when you can sit and make journal entries.

In the epigraph to this chapter, G. Lynn Nelson bemoans not being in the blue Estrella Mountains to see the sun set. After the above passage, he goes on to say, "and I am not there." But he was, wasn't he? He evoked the empty space he loves.

WEEK TWENTY-SEVEN
Owning a Place

For this quarter's first entry let's take the late poet Richard Hugo's advice in his book *The Triggering Town*: Visit a place new to you and begin to make it your own. Go there to write. This can be a new town, a cafe you never went into before, a library you haven't used before, a chair you don't usually sit in, a closet that isn't yours. Write about what you see there. If there are people, what do they say? If there are other sounds, what are they? If there are plants or animals or dust balls, what do they look like? What would the place look like at sunset and sunrise, in rain, in sunlight, snow or clouds?

SIX EXTENSIONS OF THIS EXERCISE

1. Pick a day of the year—today would be fine—and give a speech from this place. Who is your audience and what do you, inspired from being in this place, have to tell them?

2. Put yourself in this place. Breathe in and breathe out. In and out. What do you take in through your senses from this place, and what toxins do you cleanse when you breathe out? Breathe an image in, exhale a fearful restricting idea out. For example: I breathe in the image of a fringed Indian tablecloth on an outdoor table, and I breathe out the idea that the inside and outside are not one; I breathe in the image of the Stairmaster just outside the doorway, and I breathe out the idea that running in place won't get you anywhere; I breathe in the image of seed pods on the porch flooring, and I breathe out the idea that cleaning up is always necessary. Keep your list going!

3. Write to this place telling it how different it is from another

place you spend time in. Be detailed and specific. Why do you want this place to know these differences? What do you make of the differences?

4. Choose one visitor to take to this place. Write to her explaining why you want her to come to this place and tell what you are hoping she will get or help you get out of such a visit.

5. Let something inanimate in this place speak to you—an insect, a plant, a piece of furniture. What does it have to say?

6. If you were to make a state park out of this place (and there are very small state parks—where I live, The Rothchild House is the state's smallest state park) and you were going to be the park ranger, what would you think is the purpose of preserving this place? Of what interest is it to others? Write a guide for their visit telling them what is of interest and what they should think about.

WEEK TWENTY-EIGHT
Each Side a Balance

Walt Whitman wrote in *Leaves of Grass*:

Sea of stretched ground-swells!
Sea breathing broad and convulsive breaths!
Sea of the brine of life! Sea of unshovelled and always-ready graves!
Howler and scooper of storms! Capricious and dainty sea!
I am integral with you. . . . I too am of one phase and of all phases.

Whitman goes on to say, "one side a balance and the antipodal side a balance."

Choose an object that you use each day—a pen, a spatula, a TV guide, a pot, a key. Write about this object, explaining your feelings toward it. Start one sentence with "I love you because. . ." and then go on to another sentence that starts "I do not love you because. . . ." Try to fill at least one page with these alternating sentences.

SIX EXTENSIONS OF THIS EXERCISE

1. Take this mundane object you just worked with and write a "he loves me, he loves me not" piece. Imagine yourself plucking petals from a flower, one for he loves me and one for he doesn't, until the petals are all plucked and the last statement stands. But you have to supply reasons for each "he loves me" and each "he loves me not." Here's an example written about a pen: "He loves me because I take him everywhere I go; he loves me not because I often leave him in the places I have gone. He loves me because I get the best from him; he loves me not because I often don't let him give me his best for long enough. He loves me because I smile at the fine printing on his side: Alamo Car Rental; he loves me not because I have made the letters wear away over time." You get the idea. Keep it going.

2. Choose another object and praise it as if you are entirely in love with it. Walt Whitman does this in *Leaves of Grass* with the Earth:

> Press close barebosomed night! Press close magnetic
>   nourishing night!
> Night of south winds! Night of the large few stars!
> Still nodding night! Mad naked summer night!
> Smile O voluptuous coolbreathed earth!
> Earth of the slumbering and liquid trees!
> Earth of departed sunset! Earth of the mountains misty-topt!

Earth of the vitreous pour of the full moon just tinged
with blue!
Earth of shine and dark mottling the tide of the river!
Earth of the limpid gray of clouds brighter and clearer for
my sake!
Far-swooping elbowed earth! Rich apple-blossomed earth!
Smile, for your lover comes!

Write extravagantly for your front porch, the knife you chop
with, your favorite bathrobe or pajamas.

3. Imagine there is a fire or other disaster and you have to leave
almost everything behind but one of the objects you have been
writing about. You are carrying it as you leave. When someone
asks what you have taken with you, begin to tell them by writing
about what you left behind, then switch to writing, "But this,
what I carry with me, I have taken because. . . ."

4. In a poem called "Songs to Survive the Summer," former
United States Poet Laureate Robert Hass writes that death is
"everything touched casually," "all things lustered / by the
steady thoughtlessness / of human use." Write a list of such
things in your life that are taken for granted—the key in your
ignition or door lock, the road from home, the hairbursh on
your dresser. Tell the ways in which they will outlast you and
go on when you are no longer here. In this way you will bring
spirit into your life.

5. Allen Ginsberg wrote a poem entitled "A Supermarket in California" in which he imagined his hero Walt Whitman "poking
among the meats in the refrigerator" and then the two of them
walked "down the open corridors together . . . tasting artichokes,
possessing every frozen delicacy, and never passing the cashier."
Among the questions Ginsberg asks Whitman is, "Will we walk

all night through solitary streets?" and "Will we stroll dreaming
of the lost America of love . . . ?" Put somebody famous you
admire into a common scene in your life—pruning in your
garden, pulling your car into your garage, mowing the lawn,
cooking in your kitchen, cleaning or doing laundry. Name that
person and describe what you see her doing. Ask her questions.

6. Imagine you are applying for funds to create a public art
   project. Your idea is to create an art installation in a public
   place with a theme about the life of everyday objects. Describe
   your art installation—where it is, what is in it, what it looks
   like, how people come to see it, and how it conveys your ideas
   about everyday objects to viewers.

WEEK TWENTY-NINE
Recipes

We all have our favorite recipes. We all know how to make something to eat or how to repair something. What recipes have we
learned, though, for other aspects of our lives: disaster, failure, success, friendship, marriage, parenting, solitude, being a host, being
an artist, being an expert? Choose one of the above or add one of
your own, and write down directions for how to create this quality
in your life. What are the ingredients and where are they found? In
what order do you put them together and what do you have to do
to blend the mix? Any equipment or tools needed to create the
quality? How do you know when you have created what you were
after? Do you have to test the product to be sure it's ready?

SIX EXTENSIONS OF THIS EXERCISE

1. Write a letter to a magazine editor telling her why your recipe
   for this role or quality is important or entertaining for readers.

2. Imagine including this recipe in your annual holiday letter to your friends and family. Explain why you are including this recipe for the quality you are talking about.

3. Choose another quality you know how to create and write a recipe for that one.

4. Write the editor of that magazine about why she should publish this one.

5. Write the annual holiday letter that your second recipe would appear in. Be sure to tell family and friends why you are including this one.

6. Take one of your recipes and show how it can be converted to cook up an opposite quality: success turned into failure or failure into success, deep friendship turned into acquaintance-ship or acquaintanceship turned into deeper friendship, parenting into befriending, etc.

WEEK THIRTY
Private Moments

In 1992, Sandra Haldeman Martz edited a book of poems and vignettes called *If I Had My Life to Live Over I Would Pick More Daisies.* She says in her foreword that "it is often those small private moments of decision, known only to ourselves, that live vividly in our memories." This week in your entries you have the opportunity to recall and recount some of these small private moments in your life. Start by writing a list or clustering many decisions you have made recently or in the past—to get a car fixed, to sell it; to hire someone to clean the house, to clean it yourself; to call an old friend; to save some money or to spend it. Keep going. Let yourself remember the time and the details of the choices until you reach a choice you made that has deep meaning even today. Write all about it knowing you never have to tell anyone but this journal what you were deliberating about and why you chose what you chose and what you hope happened as a result or what you know has happened.

SIX EXTENSIONS OF THIS EXERCISE

1. Write about a choice someone else made for you and what your life is like because of that.

2. Write about a time you didn't take something that didn't belong to you but wish to this day you had.

3. Write about a time you did take something that didn't belong to you and what happened as a consequence of that.

4. Write about a time that someone took something from you, then write about what it would be like if you still had what was taken.

5. Write about something you wish someone would give you right now and what your life would be like if you were given this thing.

6. Write about something you wish you could give to someone else and write about what your life would be like if you could give this thing away.

WEEK THIRTY-ONE
Your Perfect Opposite

In the early 1990s, Nick Bantock wrote a trilogy of beautifully illustrated books of correspondence between Griffin and Sabine: *Griffin and Sabine, Sabine's Notebook* and *The Golden Mean*. In the books, the two people are trying to find the way to be together despite strange turns that keep them from each other's presence. In the third book of the trilogy, *The Golden Mean*, Griffin writes Sabine that a retired Jungian analyst whose home he is visiting has looked at the symbols in his artwork and noted that he is searching for his equal opposite. Finding that opposite would mean enjoying the harmony of perfect balance.

Look around and put before you three objects, from your purse or backpack, from a drawer or from the ground beneath a tree. Decide that each of these objects is a symbol for something important to you: A lipstick may be the symbol of a colorful soul inside a hard case, a comb may be the symbol for leading an untangled life and a twig may be the symbol for places of new growth. Make up the meanings of these symbols quickly and without much hesitation. Write these meanings down (you might even want to sketch the items in your entry). Next, write about each of the symbols, what they symbolize and where that has meaning in your life.

SIX EXTENSIONS OF THIS EXERCISE

1. Now let's work on that equal-opposites idea that can give us the harmony of balance. Create three more meanings for the same symbols, but this time, make them opposites of the ones you wrote about previously. In my case, based on the examples I shared, perhaps the opposites would be:

   lipstick—a center that rises outward easily
   comb—a search for treasure in so much sand
   twig—easily snapped off the main branch

   Take one of the symbols and write a dialogue between the two versions of these symbols, e.g., Lipstick 1 and Lipstick 2. Let the versions of each symbol ask each other questions about how they can do what they do and let each symbol answer. For instance:

   LIPSTICK 1 TALKING TO LIPSTICK 2: How do you let yourself out so easily? I mean, I fear the real me will melt or break off if I let myself out.

LIPSTICK 2: I like the light and I like it so much that I don't really worry about losing myself. I just think about where I am and what I am seeing. How do you stay inside that case and not get worried about the dark and all you cannot see?

LIPSTICK 1: I like the dark. In the dark I see whatever my mind creates, and I find out what all my thoughts are. I can make up my own movies in the dark, and I don't have to watch the ones everyone else is watching.

Keep your dialogue going as long as you can. Try for a full page.

2. Take a second symbol and do a dialogue like the one above.
3. And take the third symbol and write another dialogue.
4. What does the harmony of balance sound like for your sets of symbols? Look over the dialogue you wrote for all of them. Write about how two opposites each contribute to one life that is whole and rich and full.
5. Think about someone you know. Think about three things this person has around. Write about what those three things symbolize about the person's life.
6. Write about what the opposite of these symbols would be and why that person should incorporate the opposites into his or her life as well.

WEEK THIRTY-TWO
Gratitude

In *Don't Sweat the Small Stuff . . . and It's All Small Stuff,* Dr. Richard Carlson writes about the importance of being grateful for the people in your life. He says if in the morning you remember to think of someone to say thank you to, you will have a hard time feeling anything but peace. He says to remember that these people you thank can be strangers and ones who did only a small favor like letting you merge into traffic.

In this entry, cluster or think about people who you encountered recently who you might thank for their actions or presence. Was there someone who held a door open, smiled at you, led your exercise class, took without hesitation an item you wanted to return? Decide on one of these people and write a note thanking him for the act that mattered. Think about what a nice chain of events may have been inspired in your day by the action you are thanking this person for. You may have heard the idea that the movement of a butterfly's wings in one part of the world can end up a windstorm on the other side of the globe. Let the person you are thanking see the growth in your day from his one little action.

SIX EXTENSIONS OF THIS EXERCISE

1. Branch out from people for this entry. Find some animal, bird or insect to thank for some action you saw or participated in. Write about what you are thanking the creature for and why it made a difference today.

2. Branch out to minerals. What made of stone or metal might you thank for something that happened today? Write about thanking this object and how its presence made a difference in your day. Try to focus on something small and particular— a water faucet, the trim on the door of your car, the handle to hold on the bus or subway.

3. Now do this with plant life. What plant or flower can you thank today—the mold on bread, the bush by your front door where the morning paper always lands, the sunflower brought to you by a neighbor? Write about the way you are giving thanks for the presence of this plant in your life. If you are thinking of a garden, farm, yard or greenhouse, again focus on a specific plant—the orchid just now blooming in

the municipal greenhouse, the beets harvested this morning, the eucalyptus tree you see from your corner.

4. Now let's give thanks to the elements. What in the weather can you thank today? Even the worst snowstorm or accumulation of rainy days may have in them something you noticed to be thankful for. Write the snow or the rain, the wind, the sun, the moon or the humidity you experienced today. Thank it for one small act—the way your loved one's hair looked sprinkled with snowflakes, the way water beaded on your skin, the afternoon nap you took by a warm window.

5. Now let's thank the land you stand on. Write about a small gift you received today from the dirt under your feet.

6. And now the ocean, lakes, streams or even puddles in your life. Whether you are in the rainy Northwest, the Midwest's states of many lakes, the East or West coasts with oceanfront, or the Southwest with washes only sometimes filled with water, thank the water you dealt with in your life today. Don't forget the water that you drank. What happened as a consequence of the moment you are remembering or as a consequence of just now sitting down to write?

WEEK THIRTY-THREE
Shopping

Poet Jane Shore writes in a poem titled "The Five-and-Ten":

I loved to shop at the Five-and-Ten,
the Woolworth's on Bergenline,
a block away from my parents' store.
Aiming at the aisle of School Supplies,
I'd browse up and down the narrow rows. . . .

Often the stores we remember best are the ones we were brought to or discovered ourselves in childhood. When I saw a White Castle hamburger place one summer morning while staying in Royal Oak, Michigan, I was grade school-aged again, somewhere less than fifth grade, remembering David Diamond, the older boy upstairs, and how he led us all to the first White Castle I ever saw:

In Birmingham, Michigan While My Husband Consults

There's a White Castle hamburger joint sparkling in the sun
and I think of the day David Diamond, oldest kid in the apartments
of my childhood, led the rest of us to one he'd found nearby,
its shiney 1950s exterior white tiles making it appear
like a castle from a comic book.

We bought hamburgers as often as we could for a nickel;
they're still cheap, five for a dollar, and something in me wants
to gallop across the boulevard, altered slacks I've just picked up
rippling over my shoulder like a pennant.

Take the time in this entry to remember the stores and restaurants of your childhood. Remember who took you there. Remember what you saw when inside, what the adults in the store talked about and did. After you have clustered about this or brought it to your mind, start an entry describing the store. You can begin this entry as Jane Shore does: "I loved to shop at. . . ." Or you might want to start by talking about the outside of the building itself—the door, the facade, where it is on the street, what is surrounding it. How did you get there as a child? Write the details. Was the car you got out of a 1962 Chevrolet convertible or a 1952 Pontiac? What are you wearing as you go into the store? Why have you come? What catches your eye once you are in there? What are you doing?

SIX EXTENSIONS OF THIS EXERCISE

1. Write about another building of your childhood—a church, temple, school, hospital, vacation bungalow, camp cabin. Where are you in this building? What do you see and hear, taste, touch and smell? What are you hoping for? What are you afraid of?

2. Write about a street of your childhood. Why are you on this street? Where are you going? Are you alone? What do you want to happen? What are you afraid of?

3. Write about a friend's room from your childhood. Why are you there? What does it look like? What are you doing? What are you hoping for? What are you afraid of?

4. Write about a dinner of your childhood. Who is there and why are they gathered? What are you eating? What are you thinking about? What will happen after dinner? What do you want? What are you afraid of?

5. Write about a vacation of your childhood. Where have you gone and what does it look like where you are? Can you swim where you are? Ice skate? Look at museums? How different is it from home? Do you want to stay or leave? Why?

6. Write about an injury or illness in your childhood. What happened and how? What was the treatment? What was that like for you? Who helped you and who didn't?

WEEK THIRTY-FOUR
Eating With Others

In *Under the Tuscan Sun: At Home in Italy,* Frances Mayes's memoir about living in Italy, a paragraph starts:

The table is set under a shady arbor. Cold salads, cold wine, fruit, a grand cheese soufflé somehow steamed on top of the stove. Heat simmers around the olive trees in the distance. On the stone patio, we're cool. We're introduced to the other guests. . . .

Think of a time you were a guest at a table of people you didn't know. Start writing about it as Mayes does: where is the table, what is on it when you get to it, what is off in the distance or in another part of the room. Now introduce the guests—their names and what you learn about them. What are you thinking and observing as you meet each one? Write about a conversation you had with one guest and why those words stayed with you.

SIX EXTENSIONS OF THIS EXERCISE

1. Think about another meal you had with many people you know. This time start the writing with a piece of conversation. See where that leads you.

2. Think about a meal with just one other person. Describe the setting, the table, the other person, the conversation.

3. Think about a meal with no one but you. Describe the setting, the table, yourself, your thoughts.

4. Think about a meal where something embarrassing happened. Write about the embarrassing incident.

5. Think about a meal where something surprising was announced. Write about the surprise.

6. Cluster or think about meals you enjoyed that didn't occur around a table at all. Where were you? Who was with you or were you alone? What did you eat? Describe the details so the enjoyment comes through.

WEEK THIRTY-FIVE
To Thine Own Self Be True

"Write to save yourself," Athos said, "and someday you'll write because you've been saved." These words are remembered by the main character in Anne Michaels's best-selling novel, *Fugitive Pieces*.

Keeping a journal is certainly a place to write to save oneself and hopefully at times to capture the writing that comes because you have been saved. This week's entry is about both. Think of a question you were asked often by a parent, teacher or spouse that hurt or offended you: "Why are you home so late?" "When are you coming home?" "Why are you always late?" "Why can't you do anything right?" "Why can't you be like other people?" Next write a piece in which this question floats through many times and you answer it again and again with different answers. The answers can be from various times the question was asked or they may be more philosophical. Try to write for at least a page.

SIX EXTENSIONS OF THIS EXERCISE

1. Take a question you have asked or still ask others in your life. Write an entry in which you repeat this question many times and each time tell why you ask this particular question.

2. Take a question which an advertisement asks of you ("Isn't it time you . . . ?" or "Why not . . . ?" for instance), and write an entry in which this question floats through many times and you answer it differently each time.

3. Think of a question you'd love to answer, if you could answer it any way you wanted: "Mommy, why is the sky blue?" "Daddy, why do dogs bark?" Write an entry in which the question floats through many times and you answer it elaborately.

4. Think of a question you can never really answer such as,

"Why did _____ happen to me or to _____ who I love?" Write an entry with this question floating through time and each time answer the question with an "This I don't know, but this I do know." Continue with what you do know.

5. Think of a question you have about your physical world: "Why do dew drops form in the center of the lupine blossoms?" "Why do refrigerators hum?" "Why do people move mattress and box springs in pickup trucks and on tops of cars on Sundays?" Write a story that answers this question, a story like one you would tell a child. You might begin "Once upon a time . . ." if it helps.

6. Think of a question you didn't answer correctly recently in school or at work or at home. What was the question and who asked you? What did the scene look like when they asked? Why didn't you know the answer? Do you know the answer now? Does it make a difference?

WEEK THIRTY-SIX
Admonitions

In *The Romance Reader,* a first novel by author Pearl Abraham, the main character is told many admonitions by her mother, "Come lock the door behind me." "Don't open up for anyone unless you know their voice. This is a city. You have to be careful." "Remember to lock the door with the chain."

When I was a child growing up in a development of split-level homes in the new suburbs of New Jersey, my family would ride into Brooklyn, New York, about once a month to visit my parents' families who lived in brick duplexes. My mother's childhood home was on the second story, and I don't think there was a time that my grandmother didn't caution my sister and me about leaning over the windowsill lest we fall out the window. When I got my driver's license, I don't think there was a time I used the car that my father did not caution me to remember to open the garage door before I backed the car out of the garage. I have no idea why these relatives thought I might fall out a window or back into a closed door.

We all grow up with admonitions from our elders concerning our safety. And we all sometimes laugh at these cautions or, even if we know they are important, disobey them: "Don't talk to strangers." "Don't open the door to anyone when you are home alone." "Don't tell anyone who calls that you are alone." And there are so many others, whether you live in a rural or more populated area.

Write a list of the admonitions you grew up with. Select one and write about a time you either needed to remember it or disobeyed it. Either way, what happened? How did it leave you feeling?

SIX EXTENSIONS OF THIS EXERCISE

1. Write a personalized admonition for someone you know. Write to tell them the admonition and why you think it is important for them to remember and practice.

2. Write an admonition for a leader in your community or the country. What do you want to remind him or her not to do? Why? On whose behalf are you offering this admonition?

3. Think about the "rules" you learned that are actually admonitions: "Real men don't . . . ." "Ladies never . . . ." "Good friends never . . . ." "Don't let a friend . . . ." Choose one and write about when you learned it and whether you practice this rule today, break it or fluctuate between the two. Describe the ways in which you do this.

4. Write a lecture in which someone who has power over you admonishes you concerning a deed you enjoyed doing.

5. Write a lecture you'd give that person in which you stand up for doing what you enjoyed.

6. Think about an object you have an attachment to. Think about relatives or friends looking at it someday when you are not at home. Admonish them about what not to do or think when they see this object. Elaborate on why you are making this admonishment.

WEEK THIRTY-SEVEN
Six of One, Half a Dozen of the Other

The adage "It's six of one, half a dozen of the other," has had me transfixed since childhood. I'd hear my parents and other adults use these words when making a decision and understood it from their tone and facial expressions before I understood that a dozen was twelve and six was half of twelve. As soon as I understood the math, though, I liked thinking about the words. Is six really the same as half a dozen? Doesn't six imply a complete intended amount and half a dozen only some of more? So if my father, for instance, was trying to help me make a decision and started out with the idea that the choices I had were like six and half a dozen, maybe somewhere in the words themselves was a clue as to what choice I would make.

How we say something is part of what we mean.

This week's journal entries will be about sayings or sentences you associate with your parents, relatives, teachers, friends, bosses, spouses, ex-spouses, lovers and ex-lovers. Write some sentences you remember people in your life using over and over when they were discussing life situations. My Russian Jewish grandmother would rattle away in Yiddish and then in her unique version of English she would say, "But what I'm trying to bring out is. . . ." Those words lodged in my ears—"trying to bring out" of language! She meant the point she was making, but I heard more than that in her sentence. I heard that she was forging, facilitating, holding by the hand, developing as in a photograph. To this day I love those words, "trying to bring out."

After you have written many sentences, phrases and sayings of the people in your life, choose one and describe a setting in which the person is talking and saying this statement. Describe what you are thinking as you listen.

SIX EXTENSIONS OF THIS EXERCISE

1. Take another sentence or phrase someone you know used repetitively and do the same writing exercise.

2. Write a dialogue between you and the person you are thinking of. Let the person use the phrase you are remembering over and over in the dialogue.

3. Now think of nonverbal communication from particular people in your life: a gesture, facial expression, way of leaving the room, etc. Describe this communication and the particular times it was made.

4. Whether you like this gesture or hate it, picture yourself in writing taking it on as one you will make regularly or at significant times in your life. Describe yourself doing it and the circumstances in which you will be using it.

5. Write as above using a different nonverbal communication you identify with someone you know.

6. In acting class, there is an exercise called mirroring in which people pair up and initiate actions that their partner must imitate—the rolling of a shoulder, a peeping sound, a flinging of arms, a jumping up and down. Think of people you don't know but see a lot: merchants, receptionists, parking lot attendants, bus drivers, school crossing guards, paper deliverers.

And think of people you know well. Imagine doing the mirroring exercise with each of these people. The other person initiates the movements and you imitate those movements. Describe what you see being done by whom and what you do in return. Write a page about doing this mirroring exercise with the many people you are thinking of. Mix up people you don't know well with people you do know well. Always write who the people are before you tell their movements.

WEEK THIRTY-EIGHT
What It Takes

In his award-winning memoir *Angela's Ashes*, Frank McCourt writes of himself as a boy. He remembers the Friday his mother pushed a pram with his baby twin brothers along Brooklyn streets while he and his young brother walked along. She was hoping to catch his father as he came out from work on payday before he drank the money away in bars. Later that night, the young Frank is in bed with his little brothers and thinks:

> I look out at Mam at the kitchen table, smoking a cigarette, drinking tea, and crying. I want to get up and tell her I'll be a man soon and I'll get a job in the place with the big gate and I'll come home every Friday night with money for eggs and toast and jam and she can sing again Anyone can see why I wanted your kiss.

All of us remember times, especially around the age of four or five, when we wanted to take care of our parents or siblings to make things come out right. Cluster about your memories of times as a child when you wanted to give whatever it took to make things work out. Write about one or more of these times. Begin by describing yourself in a place from childhood. McCourt is in bed with his brothers looking into another room. Where are you? The back seat of the car? At the kitchen table? In front of the television set? What do you see? What are you wishing for? How are you going to make this happen?

SIX EXTENSIONS OF THIS EXERCISE

1. How did what you are writing about in the first entry actually turn out? Write at length about the behaviors and circumstances of those involved.

2. Think of a recent time when you wished you could rescue someone or make things turn out right. Describe yourself in a physical place wishing this. What are you seeing and hearing? What are you thinking you might do?

3. Think of a time you were in need emotionally, spiritually, physically or financially. Write about the straits you were in. Set the scene with details describing where you were and what you were dealing with.

4. Write about one particular person who helped during the time you wrote about. Describe the person who helped. What did he or she do?

5. Describe the changes in your life or situation that resulted from the help offered to you.

6. What help would you like most right now in your life? Write a letter to yourself asking yourself to rescue you. What does that rescue entail?

WEEK THIRTY-NINE
Self-Reflection Week

Turn back to the last week of entries from the second quarter. Consider the goals, advice or plans you wrote about as the boss concerning the journal keeper and as the journal keeper responding to the boss.

Next look over this current quarter's entries and think about whether you managed to address the concerns you had at the end of the second quarter. Write about this from the journal keeper's point of view and then from the boss' point of view. Are these two enjoying working together? Are there new goals to be set for the journal keeper and her writing or old goals still to be satisfied?

SIX EXTENSIONS FOR SELF-REFLECTION

1. Look back over several entries. Check for use of details. Find a place where you could have used more detail to describe someone, something or some event. Take the time now to write the details. Write about how you feel about your writing and your subject after experiencing the details you now put on the page.

2. Reread your twelve weeks of entries. For each week apply metaphorical thinking to describe the attitude you are picking up from your writing. For instance, you might write: "Week 1: I sound screechy like fingernails across a chalkboard. Week 2: I experience myself as the new moon hidden by mountains. Week 3: My spirit seems to have risen like a full moon against a clear sky."

3. Take one of the metaphors you created and write more about the self you experience in this way. If I chose the metaphor about sounding screechy, I would think about other times in my life that I might have had this tone. I'd describe at least one scene where this was true and then maybe just list others.

4. Take a second metaphor you created and write more about yourself as seen through that lens.

5. And choose a third metaphor you created and write about that way of experiencing yourself.

6. You've considered three yous in the last three entries. Write about what you are going to do with this knowledge about yourself.

∞

A third quarter of keeping a journal done and accomplished! It is time to celebrate three-fourths of a year of writing. What feels good? A meal out in a restaurant (and be sure to bring a matchbook home to paste in your journal), a party with other journal keepers (you can have a little reading from the journals if you feel like it), a movie in which writing matters (*23 Charring Cross Road* or *The Dead Poet's Society* or *Henry Fool* might be good to rent.)

Whatever you earmark or plan as a celebration, paste something (that matchbook or a photocopy of a videotape cover, for instance) into your journal that will remind you of the pleasure you had celebrating your accomplishment.

And now, on to the final thirteen weeks of the year!

CHAPTER EIGHT

Fourth Quarter

We know more than we can say: we live
in waves of feelings and awareness
where images unfold and grow
along the leafwork of our nerves and veins.

PETER MEINKE
"Azaleas"

Here you are at the beginning of the last quarter of a year of journaling. You have written so much, yet there will always be so much more to write and so much more to keep you writing. Close your eyes a moment and think of Peter Meinke's image: "the leafwork of our nerves and veins." Imagine all the experience carried in and along those lines, how it recirculates and how it feels the same and different each time it passes through.

In the first week's entry this quarter, you will have a chance to combine two "awarenesses" and mine both of them for new understanding.

First You Have to Teach a Lesson

In Paula Vogel's Pulitzer Prize-winning play, *How I Learned to Drive*, the main character enters, stands center stage and addresses the audience. "Sometimes to tell a secret, you first have to teach a lesson," she announces. The lesson the play uses as its central theme is one about driving—the connective tissue of the play is made up of quotes from a manual for getting a driver's license in the state of Maryland and images and dialogue about driving. The secret that the central character will tell is about an inappropriate yet loving relationship between herself and the married uncle who she saw as a father figure and who saw her as a substitute for his wife. He taught her to drive. He taught her his love of driving. And it is a good thing she has that love of driving and of feeling her own strength; his power over her as a young woman and his death from alcoholism when she said she couldn't marry him weigh heavy on her conscience.

To begin this journal entry, cluster a number of topics around the circled word, *lesson*. What lessons have you learned? Don't think about big life lessons right now, but skill sets—driving, swimming, baking, mountain climbing, hiking, pruning trees, guitar playing, piano playing, ballet, weaving, watercolor, etc. Let yourself freely associate to find one lesson that interests you today as you write. Now write about that lesson or the series of lessons it took to learn the skill. What did you learn? What were the steps in the lesson? Who taught you and what do you remember about that person?

When you are done writing about the lessons and the teacher, think about secrets you have. Do a cluster if you feel like it. Write a short paragraph about this secret.

End your entry with the words: "I could tell you about _____ (fill in the secret you wrote about) if I taught you how to _____ (fill in the lesson you wrote about above)."

SIX EXTENSIONS OF THIS EXERCISE

1. You might find that talking about learning to swim could enable you to talk about your secret wish to be an astronaut. You might have said a lesson on baking would allow you to

talk about your fear of getting pregnant. Perhaps a lesson about pruning trees would help you tell a secret about your feelings about your boss. What little part of the secret could you tell along with each part of the lesson? Write those parts of the secret under the headings of the steps in the lesson.

For baking bread, for instance, the steps might be to gather the ingredients, mix them, let the dough rise, punch the dough down, bake the bread, eat it. If I was writing about the fear of getting pregnant, I would write small parts of my secret fear under each heading: "gather the ingredients" might lead to a discussion of who I am lovers with or of my relationship with my husband vis-à-vis babies and birth control; "mix the ingredients" might lead to a bit of the secret involving forgetting or purposely not using birth control; "let the dough rise" might talk about the period of time I am waiting to find out if I am pregnant, and so on.

2. What do you want to say to anyone else who holds a similar secret? Do you have something you can teach them about what to do or not to do?

3. Paula Vogel says in interviews that she uses humor in her play so her audience will laugh and drop their defenses to the painful subject matter and allow more of her characters' plight into themselves. What can you write about your secret that is funny or entertaining or amusing in some way?

4. If something nonhuman had the same secret as you, what would that be—what animal, mineral, tool, weapon, food, etc.? Write an entry from the inanimate object's point of view that tells that object's similar secret.

5. Who would hate this secret? Create a dialogue in which you divulge your secret to this person and she responds in the way you would anticipate.

6. Take the same secret and the same person and create a dialogue in which that person reacts quite differently than you would think.

WEEK FORTY-ONE
Self-Portrait, Self-Portrait on the Wall

One of my essay-writing students, Keith Van Tassel, wrote a line in which he despairs, "Ms. Failure paints her own self-portrait, then hangs it on a wall in your world without asking permission." He was speaking of a place, he told us, where "my head was . . . not facing the realities of the world." The rest of us in the group (all women) wondered why Failure was personified as a woman. We were uncomfortable with this, but Keith was clear that for him, failure was in the persona of a woman. We wondered what that self-portrait looked like.

For this week's entry, name qualities in your life like desire, the blues, knowledge, skill, anger, success, happiness, fulfillment or fear. Choose one of these qualities and imagine the self-portrait it would paint or collage or draw or photograph. What is in the picture? What media is it done in and what are the colors? What kind of a frame does it have? What wall in what room of your house is this self-portrait hanging on? When was it hung?

SIX EXTENSIONS OF THIS EXERCISE

1. Let the quality you described talk to you while it is hanging its self-portrait on your wall. What does it have to tell you about itself and its picture and why it's bringing the picture to your place?

2. Choose a different trait and repeat the entry about the self-portrait.

3. Again, write a dialogue with this trait telling you about its self-portrait and why it is now in your house.

4. And write about a third trait and the self-portrait.

5. Now write the dialogue in which the trait informs you about why it's made its self-portrait this way and brought it to your house.

6. Choose one of the traits you've been writing about. Let it tell you where it's going now that it has hung its self-portrait in your place. Let it be particular. Write something like Maya Angelou writes in *Wouldn't Take Nothing for My Journey Now* when she says:

> One afternoon, I entered Terry's to find myself surrounded by well wishers with wide smiles and loud congratulations.
>
> The bartender showed me the *New York Post* and then presented me with a huge martini. I was featured as the newspaper's "Person of the Week." The regulars suspended their usual world-weary demeanor, giving hearty compliments, which I accepted heartily.
>
> Eventually the toasters returned to their tables and I was left to grow gloomy in silence. . . .

WEEK FORTY-TWO
Bridges of Your County

In 1992, Robert James Waller published his novel *The Bridges of Madison County* which tells the tale of a farm wife and mother and her sudden midlife passion and affair with a photographer who comes through her hometown to photograph the rural bridges. The novel begins when the narrator, an author, tells of two grown children, Carolyn and Michael, who come to him with their mother's journals and old magazine clippings and documents they found with the journals after her death that tell the story of this surprising affair. They want him to write her story. He agrees to write it based on his feeling that the gentle love story would benefit a callous world where love is for convenience.

I don't know that I agree with the narrator's assessment of the current place of love in our world, but I think the title of Waller's book and the love interest's profession as photo essayist are great choices for his story. Nonetheless, the title invited satire where I live, e.g., "The Slugs of Whatcom County" was a parody title that floated around when the book was a best-seller. Your entry this week may turn into satire or a serious entry.

What do you know about in your city, town, county or state that is of botanical, zoological, architectural or geographic interest? Skyscrapers, mountains, foxes, hawks, automobile plants, cement mixers? Cluster for a while and choose one feature. Then do a freewrite called "The _____ of _____" as in "The Skyscrapers of King County," "The Cacti of Southern Arizona" or "The Cement Mixers of Snohomish." In this freewrite, imagine a trip in which you intend to visit specimens of whatever you have named to create writing, photographs, paintings or sketches. Where are you going, in what order and what do you plan to see? What will you do with the work you create?

SIX EXTENSIONS OF THIS EXERCISE

1. Think of a person you would like with you on this trip to guide or assist you or to witness it. Write a letter of invitation to this person explaining why you need the companionship.

2. Write about a surprise event you imagine happening on your trip.

3. Write to someone who was always disappointed in you telling

what you've discovered by looking at the structures or things you visited.

4. Write to a mentor or teacher you admired, telling her about one of the structures or things.
5. Of what other trip does this made-up trip remind you? Describe the real trip and tell why you are thinking about it.
6. Write to an imagined pen pal from the area you have visited—a worker in the office tower, a ranger in the Saurgo National Monument, a truck driver from the cement plant. Tell the imagined pen pal what you would hope for in a correspondence with her and what you can offer in such a correspondence.

WEEK FORTY-THREE
Sacredness in Everyday Life

In his book *Care of the Soul,* Thomas Moore writes about a client he saw in counseling who was having problems with food and dreamt that her esophagus was made of plastic and wasn't reaching her stomach. Moore says:

> The esophagus is an excellent image of one of the soul's chief functions: to transfer material of the outside world into the interior. But in this dream it is made of an unnatural substance that stands for the superficiality of our age, plastic. And if this soul function is plastic, then we will not be fed well. We will feel the need of a more genuine means of bringing outer experience deep inside us.

"The soul," Moore says, "feeds on life and digests it, creating wisdom and character out of the fodder of experience."

For this week's journaling exercise, think of your body parts, whether they are for digestion, locomotion, weight bearing, inspiration or sensing. Do a cluster of organs and parts of your body in which you assign materials, unnatural or natural, of which you say the body parts seem made: eyes like glass marbles, fingers like seaweed, calf muscles like stones, intestines like a coil of jute rope, hair like a tattered flag in the breeze. When one of the particular parts or organs and the image you have of it strikes you as worth investigating, do a freewrite. For example, I might begin:

When I caught a glimpse of myself in a shop window, I saw my hair blown back by the wind. It looked like a tattered flag, like something left up a pole and never tended to. And I thought about my hair and how I'd neglected to get it cut. But I thought about myself as the pole, out in any weather, straight and strong. I was glad for what I'd brought myself to Arizona to do. I was. . . .

SIX EXTENSIONS OF THIS EXERCISE

1. Do a similar cluster about someone you care about very much. Write a freewrite on the organ or body part and what material you have found it made of.

2. If you had to say that the people of your community are suffering because a part of them is made of the wrong material, what part would this be and what symptoms indicate the material is what you say it is? For instance, when you look at people's eyes behind sunglasses are you tempted to think you don't see eyes at all, but cursors like on a computer screen? What happens as a result of people walking around not with eyes but with cursors? What place is the cursor holding?

3. Think of the ways the people of your community are made of strong stuff. Write about it by designating a particular

organ or body part that you can say is made of something particular. Name the stuff and show how it is viable for enhancing the people and the community.

4. If you could, figuratively speaking, give your "best" organ to someone in particular who is having difficulties, what organ would it be and why would it help this person?

5. If you could receive, figuratively speaking, a organ from someone else, what would it be, from whom and why?

6. Identify a strong organ in your body and one you feel is weaker. Let them speak to each other in a dialogue where the weaker one is asking the stronger one how he/she keeps so strong. Write about the information in the exchange.

WEEK FORTY-FOUR
Hide-and-Seek

In *All I Really Need to Know I Learned in Kindergarten*, Robert Fulghum writes about hiding too well—of a kid in a pile of leaves in his front yard who doesn't get found by the seeker. He likens this hiding too well to a doctor he knew who was dying of cancer but never told anybody because he didn't want to make things difficult for those who loved him. In the end, his approach did make things difficult, though, because his family was angry he hadn't trusted them and angry he didn't say good-bye. Fulghum says he likes the game Sardines better than hide-and-seek. In Sardines, when you find the one who is hiding, you climb into the hiding place, too, and the next one to find the place does the same and so on until so many people are in there, someone giggles and the whole pack is found.

In your journal this week, write about a childhood game that took place in your house, on your front porch, in your car, on your block, in a neighbor's yard, on the school yard, in a basement, ravine or athletic field. Describe the game—who played, what you were to do, how you did it. Describe the end of the game: How did you know who won? Were you often happy or unhappy with the results?

SIX EXTENSIONS OF THIS EXERCISE

1. Describe a game you watched other children or adults play when you were a child. What did you make of this game? Did you want to play or were you hoping you'd never have to? Write about what you thought you'd be called on to do.

2. Write about a game you play now as an adult. Is it like any game you played in childhood or nothing like any of them? Tell about the likeness or the difference.

3. Take your family, the one you grew up in or the one you are in now. Think of a game you are going to have the family members all play, preferably a game they have never played. Write telling each player where to sit or stand and what to do. In other words, coach them.

4. Remember a board game from your childhood: Candyland, Monopoly, Parcheesi, Clue, etc. Describe the board and the board pieces. Describe where the game was kept and where it was played. Describe yourself physically while you played—where and how you sat, what the dice and the game pieces felt like in your hand, what you imagined while you were playing.

5. Think of a game you can no longer play for whatever reason, e.g., the equipment is broken or you can't afford it, you aren't able to find a team, your body can't move that way anymore, you don't have time. Have the game talk to you telling you the ways in which it misses you.

6. Think about someone who is suffering a disappointment or a loss or who is having a hard time. Think about a game you think that person could play to help recover happier feelings. Describe how and where to play the game and what is needed. What will the person you are telling about this game begin to notice and talk about?

WEEK FORTY-FIVE
Whistling

Last night I watched a commercial for health insurance. A young boy is playing in a lake, using an inner tube, jumping off a dock. His father is speaking about why he has extra health insurance. Among the reasons is, "I still have to teach him to whistle." In a writing group I facilitated just before that, one writer shared an essay about her elderly mother who wouldn't keep her hearing aid turned on while they watched an important golf tournament because the wind whistled too loud in her ears when it was on. In a novel by Elizabeth Evans called *Carter Clay*, Carter thinks about the TV show *Lassie* from the 1950s and the whistling that played sweetly over the credits. He remembers that hearing this whistled tune was what made him want to learn to whistle. His father, though, forbade his whistling in the house. Instead, he whistled up the alleys, and when he whistled the *Lassie* song he liked to think his family was just under an evil spell and if it could be lifted, they would all be wonderful people.

Write about the place of whistling in your life. Or of a song or humming or playing of a musical instrument when you were young—flutophone, toy xylophone, kazoo or harmonica. Why did you make this music and what did making it feel like for you? How did people react to you?

SIX EXTENSIONS OF THIS EXERCISE

1. Think about someone you knew when you were young who whistled, hummed, sang, strummed a guitar or ukulele, or played the accordion or an orchestral or band instrument. Write what you remember of this person's playing an instrument.

2. Think of a time someone's music making especially mattered to you. What were they playing? Where were you? What was special to you about this music making?

3. Think about an instrument you thought to play or musical activity you thought to participate in, but have abandoned, whether for years, months or only a few weeks or days. Let the instrument write you a letter about what life has been like since you abandoned it.

4. Invite this instrument back into your life. Write your invitation and tell the instrument what you'd like to make up to it and how you are going to do that.

5. Let the instrument write back to you. Is it accepting or declining your offer?

6. If the instrument is accepting your offer, write about the first time you get together. If the instrument is declining your offer, write about your acceptance of its decision.

WEEK FORTY-SIX
Starvation Hill

In a poem called "Starvation Hill," poet Emily Warn writes about an abandoned house:

> it sinks first onto its back porch
> as if sitting on its heels.
> Its dark pupils stare at the sky.

The poem's readers are drawn closer to the old house because the house seems, in its collapse, to be in a physical position a person might assume alone on a hill, perhaps in a moment of searching the heavens.

In Anne Lamott's book *Traveling Mercies: Some Thoughts on Faith*, the author reports a therapist asking her to describe what hunger feels like. In that moment, she realizes she can't describe it. She will search for a way to describe it.

One way to evoke a description is to give the intangible or inanimate human or animal characteristics. Another way is to compare the intangible to an object that could represent it. Is loss an angry woman? Is the wind a bird? Is fear a mole? Is accomplishment a kite?

Think about what you experienced today both through your senses and through your emotions. Do a cluster if you like. Choose one thing or feeling you experienced and compare it to an animal, person or object. Open your entry with a statement, e.g., "Loss is an angry woman waving her arms and stomping her feet." Go on comparing the experience to what you have stated it is like. After you have fully evoked the thing or being you are comparing the experience to, tell the story of how you came to experience what you did.

SIX EXTENSIONS OF THIS EXERCISE

1. Write in this way about a physical or emotional childhood experience.
2. Write in this way about a physical or emotional experience you have in a particular place whenever you go there.
3. Write in this way about a physical or emotional experience you have with a particular person.
4. Write in this way about a physical or emotional experience you have when you touch or look at a particular object.

5. Write in this way about a physical or emotional experience you have when you smell a certain smell.

6. Write in this way about a physical or emotional experience you have when you hear a certain sound.

Getting Here

In his collection of poems, *Getting Here*, Fred Weiner includes a poem dedicated to his father upon his seventy-third birthday. It is called "My First Trip to Florida," and in the poem, Weiner remembers being a kid watching his parents in the front seat—"hand resting / across the top of the seatback fingertips touching / mother's shoulder." He remembers the stops along the way—"roastbeefsandwiches browngravy whitebread mashedpotatoes / hamburgers and frenchfries glasses of milk or pepsi / pancakes in restaurants adjacent to motels." He remembers changes in the scenery—"until we saw the first palm trees. . . ." He remembers his grandfather waiting for the family's arrival and his grandfather's dog running in circles. He remembers the children running and his mother's laughter.

What trips do you remember taking as a child with someone who matters to you today? Write about the trip by showing the details you took in while en route—the ones about the vehicle or train or plane. Continue with the details you remember about food, sleep and resting on the way. Then write about how you knew you were there—what you saw, heard, tasted, smelled and touched.

SIX EXTENSIONS OF THIS EXERCISE

1. Think about a commute you do each day, an errand you run frequently or an appointment you keep regularly. Write about the route you take in the same way as you wrote about the

trip from your younger days—what it looks like in the car,
bus or subway, what you do along the way (listen to songs
on the radio, sneeze, brush your hair, etc.), what you see when
you know you are closing in on your destination and what
you see when you are there.

2. Do this same kind of writing about a route inside your house.
   Pretend you are being transported around by some vehicle,
   e.g., a toddler's hot wheel, a vacuum cleaner or a flying carpet.

3. Take a walk outside or in your house. Notice some sense
   impression that reminds you of another place you've walked.
   What color, shape, object, sound, texture or smell reminds
   you of another walk you've taken? Or what touches your skin
   as it did on another walk? Is there a taste in your mouth as
   in another time? Decide on one sensory association and describe both walks—the one you are on now and the one you
   are remembering.

4. Take a different walk and choose another sense impression
   you are having. Write about another time and place you associate with this sense impression.

5. Think about some cooking smells you experienced during the
   day. Describe those smells, then choose one and write about
   a time and place somewhere else that you associate with those
   smells. For instance, a friend who grew up in Taiwan told
   me when she smells garbage she feels happy because it brings
   back the whole city of Taiwan where garbage smelled but her
   life was good. The smell of garbage brings back a colorful life.

6. Now take a ride or walk around your own mind and describe
   a map of your mind. There must be areas of obsessions, areas
   of knowledge, areas of ignorance, areas of obligations, etc.
   What are the streets and avenues called? Where do they lead
   or dead-end? Are there freeways in some of the areas and

windy rural roads in others? What buildings and landscapes are there? What places do you know how to get to with your eyes closed and what places require directions? Give yourself directions to a new place in your mind.

WEEK FORTY-EIGHT
Bureks

Poet Charles Simic writes in "Food and Happiness," one of the essays in his book *The Unemployed Fortune-Teller:* "I have to admit, I remember better what I've eaten than what I've thought." With these words, though, he begins, via describing the food in his life, to tell about the learning in his life. He writes that at age nine he learned there "was more to food than just stuffing yourself." He ate a *burek*, phyllo dough stuffed with ground meat, cheese or spinach. It was made by Dobrosav Cvetkovic who watched Simic eat it, studying him, Simic writes, like a cat studies a bird in a cage. Simic realized Cvetkovic wanted his opinion, and he told the baker that he must know something other *burek* makers did not. Simic calls this his first "passionate outburst to a cook." He writes about himself at thirteen, while on a seaside trip, hanging around with the sixteen-year-old daughter of the innkeeper whose meals were delicious:

We used to swim out to a rock in the bay where there were wild grapes. We'd lie sunbathing and popping the little blue grapes in our mouths. And in the evening, once or twice, there was even a kiss, and then an exquisite risotto with mussels.

Lest you think it is only exotic food Simic loves, he writes also about coming to America and eating bags of potato chips in front of the TV with his brother while his parents approve of their being American. He writes about his awe when visiting the neighborhood supermarket for the cans and packages of deviled ham, marshmallows, Spam, Hawaiian Punch, Fig Newtons, V8 juice, Mounds Bars and Planter's Peanuts. He writes of meals with Sicilian friends and a "heightened consciousness" as he remembers the linguine with anchovies.

For your journal entry this week, cluster around the word *food.* Think of food around which you have pleasure and a rush of memory. When you have located a food image that you want to write more about, do a freewrite describing where this food came into your life. Show the scene as you remember it.

SIX EXTENSIONS OF THIS EXERCISE

1. Some food is definitely connected in our minds with feeling illness or with unhappiness. I remember the smell of relish in my tuna fish sandwich as I walked home from school before lunch with a terrible earache. I remember the greenish cast of the baked eggs my mother served two hours late because my sister and I refused to stop playing outdoors. Cluster around the images of food you have not enjoyed. Write about the event, the food and the sensation when you were around that food.

2. There are rituals around food—communal preparation, prayers, particular food for particular holidays or family events. Think about food and the rituals involved with it, ones you remember from childhood. Describe the rituals, the food and the people involved.

3. Where is the most peculiar place you ever had something to eat? Describe this place, yourself and others in it, and the food.

4. Write about a time you received food most unexpectedly—a treat, a gift, a sharing.

5. Think about cliches people use concerning food and eating: "Your eyes are bigger than your stomach." "Finish what's on your plate because the people in China are starving." "I have enough food here to feed an army." Take one of the cliches you remember hearing and write about particular times it was said and what you did and thought.

6. Think about how we use food or eating images in cliches about behavior: "I'll wash your mouth out with soap." "I'll make you eat your words." "Don't make a meal of it." What was one cliche or expression involving food or eating you heard often in your life? Who said it? When? What were you doing?

WEEK FORTY-NINE
Here Lies My Heart

Writer Lewis Buzbee's essay "This is My Last Affair" appears in an anthology entitled *Here Lies My Heart*. He writes about his telephone:

THE TELEPHONE rests on a bookshelf next to my desk, lifeless plastic and wires. It was one of the first gifts she gave me, and for a year and a half it appeared as volatile and menacing as a handgun. I'd wait for it to explode. And when it did ring, I'd pick up, never knowing whether she'd say, "Come see me right now," or, "It's all over."

What is your telephone like to you? Menacing as a handgun or bubbly as water from a fountain? Quiet as a stagnant pool or persistent as a fire alarm? Write about your telephone in your life today. Start out as Buzbee does with the words "THE TELEPHONE" capitalized, and show where it is and how you perceive it. Buzbee goes on to talk about the affair he was having. Your writing about your phone will lead you to writing about what is at the heart of why your phone seems the way it does.

SIX EXTENSIONS OF THIS EXERCISE

1. Choose a different appliance—your stove, oven, microwave, TV, stereo, toaster, mixer, alarm clock. Do the same exercise.
2. Think about your car or method of transportation (train, bicycle, bus, your own two feet) and do the same exercise.
3. Think about the coat you usually wear when it is cold or chilly. Compare this coat to something as you have the telephone, appliances and method of transportation.
4. Think about a coat you wore as a child and do the same exercise from the child's point of view.
5. Think about a toy or a treasured object you had as a child. What can you compare it to? Write about this toy or object in the same way as you have been writing this week.
6. Think about an environment you were in a lot as a child—a health club swimming pool, a school hallway or classroom, a room in your house, a place under a streetlight, a waiting room, a porch or a doorway. Compare this space or environment to something else and write as you have in this week's exercises.

WEEK FIFTY

Scenes

Nobody likes a scene, we are told. Don't make a scene. I certainly operated from this thought when on a trip to Paris. My husband, who could speak only a few words of French, was angry at a cafe waiter for bringing him a well-done steak when he had ordered his rare. "*Tres rouge,*" he had said many times in ordering. The steak brought to him was very brown. To my dismay, my husband began complaining right there at the outdoor, linen-covered table with a view of the Eiffel Tower. "*Pas rouge. Pas rouge,*" he said over and over to the waiter, who pretended not to understand my husband's complaint. My eyes were down, my cheeks *tres rouge.* Finally, the waiter took the steak and served my husband another just the way he had wanted it.

No one likes a scene, we say, and admonish others not to make one. But I felt proud of my husband for insisting and not letting someone willfully tease him. We all enjoy the parts in movies, plays and TV shows where the person we identify with speaks up to a partner, a bully, an unfair bureaucrat, or oppressive generals, teachers, politicians or bosses. I think courtroom scenes are the epitome of this need to see the right side speak up. The lawyers get to make the case we all want to hear in one big scene.

How many times have you thought of all the things you would have liked to have said or done in a situation only when it was too late? Here's a chance to write yourself into the scenes you would have liked, or still want, to play.

Cluster around the phrase, "Speak up." Think of various times you wished you had spoken up. Cluster around those times the things you would have liked to have said. Choose one of these and write a scene in which you do speak up and say and do the things you wish you had. Imagine this scene is on a movie screen. What else is in the picture? Where are you and the others in this scene? What are you saying, doing and thinking? What are they saying and doing? What happens?

SIX EXTENSIONS OF THIS EXERCISE

1. Remember a scene you witnessed as I witnessed the one with my husband in Paris. Describe the scene in detail and with

dialogue if there was any. What did you feel at the time? Describe your feelings as you write about it now.

2. Yesterday afternoon I watched *The Rosie O'Donnell Show* on TV as I cooked for company. Barbara Walters was a guest on the show and she was talking about her recent interview with Elizabeth Taylor. When Rosie asked Barbara how Liz was, Barbara asked her if she remembered the scene in the movie *When Harry Met Sally* when Sally orders food at a restaurant and pretends to have an orgasm while eating it. Ladies from the next table say to the waitress, "Give me what she's having." On the air, Barbara reported Liz is feeling so good all Barbara wanted to say was, "Give me what she's having."

   Think of a scene you remember well from a movie or TV program. Describe it as fully as you can. Why do you think it has stayed in your memory so long? Is there an association you can make to a scene in your own life?

3. When did you make a scene that you regret making? In *Angela's Ashes*, author Frank McCourt throws up in his Irish grandmother's backyard after his communion. He sees the wafer of God there in the vomit. He has sinned, he believes, and his grandmother, he says, no longer talks to his mother and father because of how he threw God up in her backyard. Write about a scene you made and what you think people think as a consequence.

4. When did you make a scene that you are glad you made? Write about this scene and the consequences of it in your life.

5. Who do you wish would make a scene more often? Who do you know who you believe would benefit from standing up to someone or from expressing himself fully? Write this person a letter describing the scene you'd like to see.

6. Imagine a trash can where you have crumpled up and thrown

away images. There are old friends, lovers, family members at different ages, groups you've belonged to, animals, and buildings and landscapes from your travels. Imagine yourself reaching into the trash can and pulling up several images, one from each of the following categories: activities with friends, celebrations, new places, music, new clothes. Create a collage of scenes from different times in your life by writing about your particular image for each of the categories. For example, my list might be bowling in seventh grade, the champagne toast at my first wedding, moving to Illinois, "The People on the Bus" sung with preschoolers, and dyed freshwater pearls on silk thread. Write at least a paragraph about each image you have supplied.

WEEK FIFTY-ONE
Penultimate

Here is the next to the last week of writing ideas for your year's journal keeping. This is a significant week. Often the next to the last is somehow more exciting than the last—there is a suspense and anticipation that won't be there when the last is said and done.

Let's work with the term *anticipation*. Cluster around this word. What are you anticipating today as you write? Certainly the finishing of a year's journal writing, but what else? A promotion? A move? A change in your relationship status? A child, a visitor, a trip? Trying out a new recipe or a new restaurant? Starting a new exercise program? A phone call? An inheritance? An operation? Bad news about something in particular? An award? A shift in your thinking? A piece of information? A dream come true?

When something you are anticipating feels interesting, write about what you are anticipating and the details of what is happening right now as you wait.

SIX EXTENSIONS OF THIS EXERCISE

1. Write about a time earlier in your life when you anticipated something with great excitement and what happened when the anticipation was or was not fulfilled. You might write about the arrival of a baby sibling, a litter of puppies or a new bicycle. You might write about the new dress your mother told you she'd bought for you and how what you saw was nothing like what you'd imagined.

2. Write about something you would like someone else to anticipate: growing up, getting married, having children, finding a profession, traveling abroad, learning creative expression, etc. In the form of a letter, tell this person what you would wish for her and why the very anticipation of such a thing changes lives.

3. Think of words that rhyme with anticipation: constipation, trepidation, emancipation, unification, creation. Can you write about a time you were anticipating something and you experienced something of one of the words that rhymes with anticipation?

4. Think of another thing you once anticipated. Write twelve paragraphs about that time, one paragraph for each letter in the word *anticipation*. Start the first sentence in each paragraph with a word that starts with that letter in the word *anticipation*.

5. Penultimate. Imagine yourself doing something heroic. Something you believe you could really do that would help people or a particular person. Write down what that heroic action is in detail. Now imagine this heroic deed is only the penultimate step. What is the final action? Write about that.

6. Penultimate. Look at a sentence in a book, magazine, newspaper, report or advertisement. Any sentence will do. What is

the penultimate word in this sentence? Write, for a least ten minutes, on whatever comes into your mind about that word.

Self-Reflection Week

This self-reflection and evaluation of the journal keeper is the last of four you've done this year. You may deserve a raise or a rest or a new way of doing your job. Write down what you have to say to your journal keeper after this last quarter and what she has to say to you. How did using the writing ideas of the last quarter feel the same or different from other quarters? How did she feel keeping up with the journal writing? Has it become a longed for part of the day or week, or is it feeling like a chore? If it is a chore, what can she suggest to you that will help her get back to the feeling of adventure she started out with?

The journal keeper needs a job description that allows her to approach her job the way she is asking to, perhaps after a short but well-deserved vacation. Does she want to continue the journal process by beginning again at week one or by doing some of the ideas in this book she didn't use this time around? Does she want to do some research and development using the last chapter of this book and begin exploring other journaling ideas? Does she want to explore using this book in combination with other books? Perhaps the journal keeper should write her own job description this time.

SIX EXTENSIONS FOR SELF-REFLECTION

1. Look back through your journal entries this quarter. Your writing will be from many different parts and times in your life. Make a map of your life as it is expressed in the journal entries. There are peaks, valleys, meadows, swamps, oceans,

rivers, highways, industrial areas, vacation spots, etc. Draw a map that represents what you see about your life from your entries. Label the geographical places on your map after the feelings and occasions you find in your entries.

2. Look back through your entries again. Think about which entries have information that surprises you. Have you seen a sexual side of your personality or a fondness for someone you thought you totally disliked? Write about the openness these surprises indicate.

3. Look through your entries for judgmental or editorializing words, e.g., horrible, beautiful or lovely, words that tell rather than show. Take several of the sentences with these kinds of "tell" words, and write more using details that show and evoke what you are writing about rather than just telling how you feel about the subject. Reread what you just wrote. Do you have more or different feelings about the subject?

4. Joseph Campbell said that although people are always saying they are looking for meaning as in the "meaning of life," he thought they were looking for the "experience of being alive." Where do your journal entries seem most alive? Write about your experience of this aliveness and how it is transmitted from the page.

5. Reread your entries. Write down three new things you can say about yourself with conviction from reading these entries. No judgmental words allowed. Show don't tell: "I am often at a loss for words," rather than "I am a poor writer." "I am wanting to look at the bright side," not "I am a happy person." "I remember less detail than I want to," rather than "I have a lousy memory." Now take the three new things you can say about yourself and write a prescription for yourself: "I am going to learn one new word a week and practice using

it." "I am going to continue to look at things that happen until I see the gift in them for me." "I am going to practice recording detail by noting something I see in passing and three days later writing a paragraph about it."

6. We keep journals for the opportunity to honor writing as a process in our lives. We gain satisfaction and excitement from knowing we are going to be writing, from the writing and the having written. We may be delighted when we reread what we wrote, or we may be puzzled or saddened. We may smile at what we thought we had forgotten. We may cry at what we thought had been a beautiful day. Our writing cultivates our emotions; it prepares the soil, sows the seeds, waters, fertilizes and harvests them. Take a couple of the emotions you have after reading your words from this quarter. Can you trace their growth over the ten weeks of entries?

:∞:

It is time once again to reward yourself for a job well done—a whole year of journaling. Perhaps your reward is a new journal you design for yourself. Perhaps it is copying out writing from your journal that you are especially fond of so you can send it to someone or frame it. Perhaps you want to get a birthday present for the journal. What is appropriate for this young but ancient soul? You will think of it. Put it in the journal or in a room you write in.

Stand up and raise your arms above your head. Take a deep breath and slowly lower your arms as you exhale. Cross your arms over your shoulders and pat your back. Shake out your hands. It's been a long journey, full of the stillness in which everything rushes in!

When you are ready, turn to chapter ten about resources for journal keepers and to the appendices at the back of this book, full of journal entries to read and a bibliography you might find helpful.

CHAPTER NINE

Journal Writing for Life Occasions and Holidays

give me all the pain

of everyone, I'm going to turn it

into hope.

Give me

all the joys,

even the most secret,

because otherwise how will these things be known?

PABLO NERUDA
Absence and Presence

On the day of a religious or secular holiday or event, or upon a birth, death, marriage, anniversary, or upon another beginning or ending, you may want to work with a writing prompt that focuses attention on the special meaning, joy or grief of the day. Instead of using the weekly exercise or an extension, look at the following for an exercise created to help you find out what is at the bottom of your mind and heart on particular life occasions and holidays.

Eight Life Occasions

Birthdays

I remember reading a few years back that someone owned the rights to the song "Happy Birthday" and day care centers that were singing that song to celebrate children's birthdays were being fined for not paying royalties (the money exchanged for permission to use material owned by others). Every time I sing that song at a birthday party now, I feel like I'm getting away with something. It makes me think, too, that having a birthday is itself a little like getting away with something. We have used our bodies to accomplish work or for craft-making, lovemaking or childbirth; our dreams to help us find our way; our minds to make informed decisions and discoveries; and our love to connect us with family, friends and community. Choose one: body, dreams, mind or love. Think about what you might owe for your use of it and its properties. Write about this. If you were to defend yourself as a day care center might, what would you say about your need to use your mind, body, dreams or love without penalty? Write about it, and you will pay tribute to yourself and your life on this planet.

To pay tribute to someone else on their birthday, imagine your time spent as parent, grandparent, teacher, friend. Write about what the person has used of it and why there is no payment due.

Marriages

Author Bharti Kirchner opens her colorful novel, *Shiva Dancing*, with the wedding of Meena, a seven year old in Karamgar Village, India. She and her childhood friend Vishnu and eight other pairs of village children will be married this day in a traditional Hindu ceremony. Meena is thrilled to be marrying her childhood friend. She won't go to live with his family until she is fourteen. After the ceremony, the village mothers begin a "ululation of joy, punctuated by the ringing of cymbals." *Ululation* means "a howling." I think howling helps us discharge feeling when we are overloaded, either with joy or with pain or with both simultaneously. A marriage involves, as Meena already knows, the happy and the sad, for it is about change—seeking and going forward as well as leaving.

Now is a good time to write a ululation for the time of marriage. You might want to repeat the sentence "I enter this marriage (or 'you enter this marriage' if you are writing about someone else's marriage) and I howl out about. . . ." As you finish these sentences write the images of what you (or the person you are writing about) are leaving and the images of what you are moving toward. Make the words bold and loud as well as specific. Put in the ringing of cymbals here and there throughout the writing—maybe in the form of lyrics from a wedding song or prayer or words from a friend or relative. In Meena's case, the cymbal sound could be her aunt's words, "Big green eyes . . . Shiny black hair. A face like the goddess Sita's."

Divorces

In the anthology *Here Lies My Heart*, twenty-one writers tell about their marriages and divorces. William Morris writes in the title essay, "With divorce one gives up a whole way of life—friends, routines, habitudes, commitments. You are on your own again, and in diaphanous territory, and for a while your most fiendish habits may worsen."

Diaphanous describes something characterized by an extreme delicacy of form, something that can be seen through as well as something that is insubstantial and vague. Write a meditation on the word *diaphanous* to focus thoughts about a divorce, yours or that of someone close to you. Start with the word, *diaphanous*. Let yourself free associate—I hear the sound of "die after us." What dies after the "us"? Certainly the routines and habits of the marriage; it is hard to break those just because the marriage is gone. Write about those habits; write about a state in which you are a "see-through" person, write about what it means to be suddenly vague rather than substantial.

If you are writing about someone else's divorce or want to write more about your own, describe the diaphanous garment of this divorce, its delicacy of form. What is the garment of this divorce made of? What color is it? What is its function? If you were to put this garment in a store window, what store would it be? What else would be in the window dressing? Who would come to view it?

Deaths

When someone who mattered to us dies, we may more than ever need to find reasons to believe in what contemporary philosopher Sam Keen calls "a deathless and kindly higher power." If we lose someone we feel we shouldn't have to lose, it can be hard to look for and find reasons to believe. In *After Death: How People Around the World Map the Journey After Life*, author Sukie Miller quotes Keen:

> One morning as I walked to work through a park, in the middle of a large field the sky seemed to open. A voice from the infinite silence within and beyond me said: "You don't have to know." I was flooded with an immense sense of relief, as if a thousand-pound weight had been lifted from my shoulders . . . My mind reveled in the knowledge that I could never have certain knowledge of the ultimate context of my existence.

This is the beginning of Keen's understanding of hope, a knowing "that we can not know the limits of the Ever-Creating Power that has, is, and will bring all that is into being. And beyond that, we must trust that the inexhaustible mystery we touch when we discover our soul-spirit-freedom-capacity-to-transcend provides our best clue to the nature of Being."

To write about a loss due to death requires an abandoning of oneself to hope. Imagine the one you have lost going outside to look at the sky. Determine whether it is the day sky or the night sky. Write what the person who has died would find in the sky. Why would he or she have stepped outside? What land or water or building is the sky above? What would the person be reminded of looking at stars, clouds, moon, sun, airplanes, birds and bobbing satellites?

"Our birth is but a sleep and a forgetting," William Wordsworth wrote in "Ode: Intimations of Immortality from Recollections of Early Childhood." Hope as Sam Keen writes of it is our antidote to this forgetting. Writing on the skies from the point of view of the deceased is such an antidote as well.

Births

The birth of your baby, grandchild, cousin, nephew, niece or child of a friend makes the heart bubble with the newness of the new, the ongoing nature of nature. Here are lines from William Wordsworth's "Ode: Intimations of Immortality from Recollections of Early Childhood." Read them aloud and hear joy:

> The Winds come to me from the fields of sleep,
> And all the earth is gay;
> Land and sea
> Give themselves up to jollity,
> And with the heart of May
> Doth every Beast keep holiday;—
> Thou child of Joy,
> Shout round me, let me hear thy shouts. . . .

Welcome the new child into the world as Wordsworth does but write longer. What in nature came to tell you of the birth of the child? Were there specific flowers blooming, a soft rain shower softening the seeds that needed to sprout? Did you notice a butterfly or hummingbird on the child's birthday? Did a ladybug land on your arm? Did storm clouds disappear or drop their rain with force and winds? Did a rabbit hop across the road? What did your cat or dog do? The fish in an aquarium? After you have explored the specific responses of nature to this day of the child's birth, write the shouts you want to hear. What will this child shout and laugh about? Write as lengthy and specific a list as you can.

Anniversaries

In writing about an anniversary of a thirty-year marriage, Helen Trubek Glenn says in her poem "Negative Space":

> What can I do tonight except slowly stir
> the soup to keep it from crusting,
> place round spoons on linen napkins,
> pull the bread into pieces.

The images and actions of daily life speak to the work of keeping a relationship. On the anniversary you are writing about, describe what you will do this day of the anniversary. Use particular details and information that comes in through the senses because they will ultimately do the emotional informing. Like Glenn, you might want to use a question. You can repeat this question to keep yourself writing whenever you feel you need the impulse to go on in the writing: "What can I do today except . . . ?"

Endings and Beginnings

Since change is what we can count on in life, times of endings and beginnings are sprinkled through our days. Jobs and projects, honors and titles, visits and travels all begin and end, and new ones come and go. Here are two exercises you can do when an ending or a beginning fills your mind.

Upon an Ending

All good things must come to an end. Everything has its life span. What goes up must come down.

As much as we might not want something to end, it will end. A job ends because the company changes or we get fired or retire or move away. A relationship ends because one of the parties decides it is over or someone dies or moves away. Things fall apart and things go wrong and accidents happen. We all deal with endings, big and small, and more often than we'd like. And we all hope to see the phoenix of new possibility rise from the ashes of what has died.

Sad or Bitter Ending

To journal upon the occasion of a sad or bitter ending, build a metaphorical bonfire and sit by it a while. The kindling, the logs and the hot coals can each be memories concerning what has ended. Bring them to the fire, arrange them and make a big blaze. Where are you building this fire? What do you think as you are preparing it? What do you wear as you gather the wood and arrange it and then sit there? What needs stoking? What do you add to the fire? How long does it take until the fire goes out? Look at the ashes. What do you see there? What do you wish to rise from them?

Poignant or Gentle Ending

To journal upon the occasion of a poignant or gentle ending, write about a scrapbook you could make of pictures and trinkets from the event or relationship that has ended. What does the scrapbook look like? Where will you keep it? What is in it? Tell why you are placing particular photos and objects into the scrapbook. When the book is finished what will it be called? Can you find a title that tells the most important thing you get to keep from this collection of memories and experiences?

Upon a Beginning

All during our lives new relationships come into being; we start new jobs, projects and responsibilities. Longed-for vacations or living situations arrive. Imagine each beginning you want to write about personified and talking to you across a table, over drinks in the living room, on the front porch or deck or patio or in a restaurant. You are the host. What beverage does your guest want to drink? What food does your guest like for dinner or what have you prepared and why? What does "new relationship" or "new job" or "new friendship" or "trip to Italy" have to say? Is your guest happy to be with you or nervous? What are you and your guest worried about? What are you happy about? If you were to make up a toast what would it be?

Holidays and Other Observances

For any holiday, you can do a satisfying journal entry by (1) writing a short description of what the holiday commemorates and what rituals it uses to do that, (2) writing your memory of that particular holiday celebration in your past, and (3) writing new rituals to perform that will help you reflect on the meaning of this day. Following are exercises for some of the holidays in a year.

New Year's Day

When Julius Caesar changed the calendar and made January the first month of the year, Romans celebrated the new year by dancing, feasting and giving presents. After the Romans accepted Christianity a few centuries later, they began to celebrate the new year with prayer and reflection on their lives. In the 1600s and 1700s, according to Linda Polon and Aileen Cantwell, authors of *The Whole Earth Holiday Book*, the holiday ushering in the new year became a noisy one because people wanted to scare away dark spirits. Banging on drums and kettles and whistling and shouting were in order.

As you celebrate a new year, spend some time scaring away whatever "dark" you no longer want in your life. Write a description of yourself making the noises that will keep specific "spirits" away. What grieving do you want to be done with? What jealousy do you want to release from your being? What fear do you want to get rid of? What self-limiting ideas do you want to chase away? Write about this by fully envisioning yourself in a ceremony of noise-making. Are you holding a canning pot and beating it with a wooden spoon as you encircle your house or yard while you yell at the dark spirits? Who are they or what do they represent in your life? What are you saying to them? How does your voice feel to you as you yell? Your arms as you make the noise? Your feet where they are standing or stomping or walking?

If you want to write more to celebrate the new year, imagine yourself writing resolutions for yourself and/or for others. Write at least five and for each one, imagine what you might write it on and where you might hide it so it will be a surprise when it is found sometime during the year. Might you etch it into the bark of a tree? Write it on a scrap of paper the robins might snatch to use in building a nest? Might you leave it under a rock in the garden? For each of the five resolutions, write about when you or the person you are writing for will come upon the resolutions. Where is that?

What is the weather and time of day? What thoughts does the discovery of the resolution provoke?

Ramadan

Ramadan is a special month of the year for Muslims, a time for inner reflection, devotion to God and community. The Islamic lunar calendar is eleven to twelve days shorter than the Gregorian calendar so if Ramadan begins on January 20 one year, the next year it will begin on January 9.

Ramadan is a time of intensive worship when Muslims read the Qur'an, give to charity, purify their behavior and do good deeds. It is most important for Muslims during Ramadan to learn and practice self-control by fasting and refraining from sexual activity sun up to sun down. In this way their spirit ascends closer to God.

Secondarily, fasting allows worshippers to experience hunger, gain sympathy for the less fortunate and learn thankfulness for all of God's bounties. Fasting is also believed to provide health benefits and a break from rigid habits and overindulgence.

During Ramadan, Muslims prepare special food for meals to break the fast, and invite one another to share the meals. They try to read as much of the Qur'an as possible. They spend time listening to the recitation of the Qur'an in a mosque, meet for Quranic studies or for congregation prayers. Some spend the last ten days of Ramadan in a mosque worshipping God.

If you want to make journal entries commemorating Ramadan, write on different days of your thoughts during fasting. Write about breaking the fast at night, the food, the people you are with and your thoughts as you eat, and write about how prayer feels on an empty stomach. In what way does it feel different than on a full stomach? Some days, write about something you learn or remember or meditate on from your reading in the Qur'an.

Martin Luther King Day

In 1968, passionate equal rights advocate Dr. Martin Luther King, Jr., was assassinated. He is remembered vividly for a speech in which he detailed his dream of good race relations in the United States and equal rights for all men and women. After many years and much hard work, Congress passed a bill in 1983 establishing the third Monday of every January as Martin Luther King Day. In 1994, another bill established the holiday as a day to focus on community service, interracial cooperation and reducing youth violence.

If you want to write a journal entry celebrating Martin Luther King Day, think about your community—your school, neighborhood or workplace. What injustices exist and what threatens the well-being of adults and children? What kind of a dream do you have to correct this situation? Write about it.

Valentine's Day

The Romans believed that birds chose their mates around the fourteenth of February. Eventually, they decided human lovers should be honored on that date, also. During the rule of Emperor Claudius, marriage was forbidden because Claudius believed married men didn't want to go into the army. A man called Valentine was jailed for marrying people. Another Valentine who lived during Claudius's reign helped Christians, which was forbidden, and he was jailed. He fell in love with the jailer's blind daughter and cured her blindness. An infuriated Claudius ordered Valentine beheaded. According to *The Whole Earth Holiday Book*, Valentine wrote a love letter to the jailer's daughter on the morning before he died, February 14.

If you want to write a special journal entry to celebrate Valentine's Day, write a love letter in one of two ways. The first way is traditional. Write to someone you love, whether he knows it or not, and tell him the ways you love him and what you appreciate in his being. If you would like to do something a little less traditional, think of someone or something you wouldn't normally think to honor with a love letter. Remember Shakespeare's *A Midsummer Night's Dream* where Puck sprinkles a special dust over people as they sleep, causing them to fall in love with whatever or whoever they first see upon waking up? If this dust had been sprinkled on you overnight, with what or who would you be in love? Write the love letter of your life to your new love.

St. Patrick's Day

Each March 17, the Irish and their descendants around the world honor Ireland with the wearing of green, symbolizing the ancient custom of burning leaves and boughs to make the soil richer. The day took on its name in honor of Patrick, born in Wales but kidnapped to Ireland where he was sold as a slave. He escaped slavery, became a priest and bishop, and spread Christianity in Ireland. It is said he used the shamrock to explain the Holy Trinity.

If you want to write a special entry for St. Patrick's Day, get out a green ink pen and think about enrichment. Just as the boughs and leaves enriched the farming soil, so did St. Patrick's teachings enrich the people. What would you have enrich your life or the life of someone you care for? How would you make the enrichment happen?

Passover

This holiday, occurring for ten days in either March or April, commemorates the Jews' flight from Egyptian slavery. As Passover begins, Jews gather around a table for a meal called a *seder*. Food at the table includes a flat bread called *matzo* to remember the fleeing (the Jews had to cross a hot desert and had no time to let the bread that they baked for sustenance leaven); a mixture of chopped nuts and apples to represent the mortar they used as slave workers for the Pharaoh; saltwater and bitter herbs for the tears and harshness; and a lamb shank bone to remember the ways in which God slew the Egyptians to help the Jews escape. A roasted egg and green vegetables represent spring and rebirth. Today Jews not only remember their own past, but they also pray for all people in the world who are still enslaved or persecuted.

If you want to write a journal entry to commemorate Passover, think of people who are still persecuted and having a difficult time. For what group or individual could you make a gesture, no matter how small or personal, that would put some freedom into the world? What would this action be and how can you take it? What symbolic food could you put together to remind yourself and others of this thought and gesture?

April Fools' Day

In 1564, Charles IX revised the calendar, and New Year's, which had been celebrated from March 25 to April 1, was now celebrated January 1. Perhaps, since it took a long time for people all over the country to find this out, people who knew may have played tricks on those who still celebrated on April 1.

This April Fools' Day, remember tricks you played on other April Fools' Days or tricks that were played on you. Write about them. Then write to mastermind the best trick ever. Write about why you want to play this trick this year.

Easter

Today Easter is celebrated on the Sunday after the first full moon of spring to commemorate the day Jesus Christ rose from the dead.

In pre-Christian times, Anglo-Saxons celebrated a festival they named *Eostre* in honor of a spring goddess. Teutonic people celebrated the spring sun, which they called *Eastre*. As Christianity spread, the joy of Christ's resurrection and joy of the return of spring combined to be celebrated as Easter.

If you want to write a special journal entry on Easter, write about revival. What life or value would you like to see returning? What would the return be like?

Cinco de Mayo

Celebrated widely with fiestas, parades, fireworks and piñatas, this holiday commemorates the Mexican victory over the French on May 5, 1862. If you would like to write a journal entry inspired by this holiday, imagine preparing a piñata for the festival. How could it symbolize your love of your mother country or your adopted country, your town or your neighborhood? In what shape do you make this piñata? What do you put inside? What will it be like when the piñata is opened and the treasures come into view?

Mother's Day

In *Mother Journeys: Feminists Write About Mothering*, Greta Hofmann Nemiroff writes that in the Wintun culture the children refer to their mothers as "She-whom-I-made-into-a-mother." This seems an interesting point of view from which to start writing on Mother's Day whether you are a mother or a child. If you are writing about yourself as a mother, write about the ways your child or children have made you into a mother. You might want to use the litany form, repeating a sentence like, "I am she whom you have made into a mother." You can list the actions you take, the feelings you have, the observations you make and the words you speak now that you have been made into a mother. You can talk about those actions, observations and words that were part of your life when you weren't a mother and add, "But you have made me into a mother." If you are writing about your own mother, you can take the point of view of how you made her into a mother repeating the lines, "I am she/he whom made you into a mother" and "That was before I made you into a mother."

Memorial Day

In 1866, Henry C. Welles, a druggist from Waterloo, New York, wanted people to decorate the graves of soldiers who had died during the Civil War. By the early 1900s, in Memorial Day programs all over the United States, Civil War veterans gave speeches, and people sang patriotic songs and marched in parades. Today, Americans are honoring the dead of all wars on this holiday as well as remembering relatives and friends who have died.

In a journal entry to focus on this holiday, imagine a parade before those people no longer living who have served you, your family or community. You are in the parade and they are all in the grandstands. Who are the people you have put in the grandstands? What do you perform before them? How does what you perform say thank you to each of them?

Father's Day

In David Huddle's poem, "Thinking About My Father," the poet remembers his father's ordinariness and how much it matters to him: "His pleasures were fresh / things, mail just pulled / from his post office box. . . ."; ". . . there he is / at home, at his desk / in the den. . . ." The poet remembers a home movie in which his young mother hands a baby to a thin man and he feels the sensation he was wanted "right here in this world."

If you are writing about your father, write in the form of a litany about his pleasures. After you have written as long a list as you can, write an ending image, something you remember that sums up an important feeling you have about your father.

If you are a father, list your pleasures for your child or children. Be specific and let yourself range from the simple to the more complicated. When your list is long, find an image from your life with your child or children that you would like to stand for an important feeling you have about being a father. Write about that image and what it stands for to you.

Independence Day

In June of 1776, the Second Continental Congress representing the British Colonies in America met to discuss the battles of Lexington and Concord and to draft a Declaration of Independence from the British government, which had infuriated colonists by taxing them on items they needed such as glass, tea and paper. On July 4, 1776, the Continental Congress met again to vote on approving the Declaration. A crowd, waiting outside the State House to hear the outcome of the vote, broke into celebration and created huge bonfires when they heard Congress had voted in favor of independence. Today, fireworks set off after dark probably symbolize the gun and cannon battles fought to win independence from the British, as well as the bonfires of celebration.

To commemorate Independence Day in your journal, write about fireworks in your community and how they symbolize your freedom to achieve, experience and enjoy. What does it mean to you that the fireworks are as dangerous to assemble and set off as they are startling and beautiful to watch? That many people lose fingers or lives setting them off? Try to make fireworks a metaphor for the dangers and joys of freedom.

Labor Day

The first Labor Day was celebrated by some on September 5, 1882, when Knights of Labor leader Peter J. McGuire requested that the first Monday in September be a day of rest for American workers. A parade in New York City's Union Square honored the working people of America. Thousands took the day off to be in the parade, to picnic, listen to speeches and set off fireworks. The first Monday in September is now celebrated each year in America to honor workers. For many, the day also marks the end of the summer holiday season and a returning to school for America's students.

If you wish to write a journal entry about Labor Day, here are two ideas: Invent a ritual to honor yourself as a worker in America. Describe this ritual and how you can observe it. What foods, symbolic materials and activities will you use in your ritual? How will you invite people to join you in this ritual? How does the ritual honor your role as a worker in America today?

Or you might want to write about the time before you were a worker. What did Labor Day mean to you then? What was associated with Labor Day when you were growing up? Putting away summer clothes and white shoes? Closing a beloved beach house? Buying notebooks and pens and pencils for school? Who was with you? What were the things you did and talked about? Write a journal entry that describes the place, the people, the events and ideas of a typical Labor Day from your childhood. Did these rituals help you think about the honor of work or was that forgotten?

Rosh Hashanah and Yom Kippur

This holiday covers ten days in late fall. Rosh Hashanah occurs on the first two days and Yom Kippur on the last two. During this time it is believed that God opens the Book of Life so people can look at their wrongdoings and figure out how to correct them before the book is closed again at the end of Yom Kippur, the Day of Atonement. Yom Kippur is a day of fasting from sundown to sundown. The fast is broken with challah, a braided bread also served on Rosh Hashanah. The braid may stand for a ladder so prayers will reach God. The Jewish High Holy Days, as they are also called, are a time in which all members of the Jewish community are called upon to look clearly at their actions and set things right if they can. Self-reflection, honest acknowledgment and effective action are beneficial to individuals and communities.

If you want to write a journal entry during the ten Jewish High Holy Days that relates to this solemn time, use the idea behind the holiday. Write a self-assessment of things you feel badly about having done or failing to do. You might repeat a line like, "I know I have . . ." or "I regret that I . . . ." After you feel complete with the list, write another list with a repeated line like "And now I will . . ." or "To make amends I will . . . ." Try to address each of the items in the first list when you write the second list. Try for variety of levels of bigness in these transactions. Sometimes we learn more about ourselves from our small regrets and sometimes a lot of small regrets add up to something larger. It is often easier to approach small regrets before we take on larger ones.

Halloween

The idea of wearing costumes to represent scary spirits and the coming of the dark season may have its roots in Druid times when priests dressed up. Whether you are stitching or buying costumes, selecting candy to give out, carving pumpkins or making plans not to be home, you have stories to tell about Halloween's past. One of the most vivid Halloween memories I have is about ringing a bell, saying "Trick or Treat," and holding up our bags when a man opened the door and pointed to a low bookcase whose top was lined with pennies. He told us to select a penny for our bags. This was 1953, and money of any denomination just for the taking was amazing! The first of us reached for the penny. "Ow!" the child exclaimed and shook his hand in pain. Each of us in turn reached for a penny and dropped it hastily into our bags because it was so hot. When we were all done, the man pointed to the lamp he had over the pennies heating them up and said, "Trick not treat." We left realizing for the first time what we were saying with our words, "Trick or Treat."

Write about a longtime Halloween memory, costume or bag full of candy, dark side and all.

Thanksgiving

When the Pilgrims came to America and landed in Massachusetts in 1620, they planted seeds from England. Their crops did not succeed, and they might have all starved if the Native Americans had not taught them about growing native food. When the Pilgrims harvested their new crops, they held a feast. Native Americans came with food as well. The first Thanksgiving probably lasted for days. Later, George Washington made Thanksgiving a national holiday and Abraham Lincoln revived it when it fell out of favor. No matter what our background or beliefs, we give thanks together as a nation for the resources that sustain us—food, shelter, jobs, friends and loved ones.

One Thanksgiving, my mother read about a ritual in the local newspaper and asked if we could do it at our table. We passed around a plate of dried beans and everyone took one. Then we passed around a cup and everyone in turn told what they were thankful for this year and dropped their bean into the cup. There was fulfillment in the sound of the beans dropped into the cup, in the different voices around the table, and the symbol that thanks were mounting. As I write this, I realize we could say our thanks only amounted to a "hill of beans." But that would be very untrue. These beans were endowed with the hearts and souls and minds of our family and friends. Each thank-you you have inside joins with other thank-yous and creates a universe of thanks and a cup that runneth over. If you want to write a special journal entry for Thanksgiving, write what you are thankful for. Figure out what you could place in a cup—a seed, an item you cherish or something funny—to create your cup full of thanks. You might want to use a sentence like, "I place clover leaf into this cup of thanks. With clover leaf I remember how I am grateful for what has created the nutritious soil of my life . . . ."

Hanukkah

King Antiochus ruled Palestine two thousand years ago and banned the practice of Judaism. Mattathias and his son Judah led Jews to defy Antiochus. Judah's army eventually defeated Antiochus and the Jews returned to Jerusalem and took their temple back. Needing to burn an eternal light to rededicate the temple to God, they found only enough oil for one night. Yet that one night's oil lasted the full eight days until new oil could be made. Hanukkah, the Festival of Light, celebrates this miracle. To symbolize the miracle, a special candleholder, the *menorah*, holds eight candles plus one called the *shammash*, or servant candle. The shammash is used to light one candle the first night, two the second and so on until, on the last night of Hanukkah, all eight candles plus the shammash burn.

If you want to write a special journal entry to celebrate Hanukkah, either the first night or all of the eight nights, imagine that you are the shammash candle, the one used to light the others. On the first night, each night or on the last night of Hanukkah, write a journal entry that "enlightens." This can be about the importance of being able to worship in a tradition that is yours, or it can be about people who have helped you get where you are, just as Judah helped the Jews get their temple back. Describe yourself or your religious observance as a flame igniting other flames, or illuminating or casting a shadow by which you or others learn. Or write about someone or ones who acted as that flame for you.

Christmas

Christmas honors the birth of Christ, born in a stable because his mother, Mary, and her husband, Joseph, were turned away at the inn. In the year 325, December 25 was chosen as the exact day to worship Christ's birth. Because of the stories surrounding the happenings at Christ's birth and because the customs of winter holidays were already well celebrated, there are a lot of traditions in the Christmas celebration based on giving, enjoying the season and honoring Christ and humanity.

Today people buy prewritten greeting cards or write letters they can mass-mail with good news about each family member. These cards and letters sometimes include a current picture of the family. This may derive from a custom of the 1800s in England, where school boys sent something they called "Christmas Pieces" to their parents to display their best writing skills.

Perhaps a fitting journal entry for this holiday would be a heartfelt "Christmas Piece" addressed to one's parents, living or dead, demonstrating your skill at telling them what Christmas has come to mean to you. Imagine a picture you would include that supports what you are writing about. Tell them in your writing what that picture is and why you have included it.

Kwanzaa

Scholar Dr. Maulana Karenga established a winter holiday celebration using the Kiswahili language, for African Americans to honor Nguzo

Saba, The Seven Principles, which serve as guides for daily living: *Umoja* (Unity); *Kujichagulia* (Self-Determination); *Ujima* (Collective Work and Responsibility); *Ujamaa* (Cooperative Economics); *Nia* (Purpose); *Kuumba* (Creativity); and *Imani* (Faith). On the evening of December 31, Kwanzaa Karamu is held for cultural expression as well as feasting. Everyone brings something or helps make the dinner. An African motif includes the colors black (the people), red (bloodshed and struggle) and green (the bountiful motherland of Africa and the hopes and dreams of black youth). Songs and group dancing, poetry, chants and unity circles are often performed.

There are seven objects used in the evening's celebration: *Mazao*, crops like fruits and vegetables, symbolize the rewards of collective labor. *Mkeka*, a place mat, is the symbol of tradition and history. *Kinara*, a candleholder with candles called *Mishumaa*—three green, three black and three red—symbolizes the continental Africans, African-Americans' parent people. *Vibunzi*, ears of corn, represent the number of children in a family and their potential as producers and reproducers. *Zawadi*, gifts, are a reward for commitments that are made and kept and exchanged between members of a nuclear family. These gifts are educational and often handmade so no one falls victim to commercialism. There is also a *Kikombe Cha Umoja*, or communal unity cup, at the meal. A *Nguzo Saba*, which has the seven principles printed in large letters, and the *Bendera ya Taifa*, the national flag of black, red and green, are also often incorporated into the event.

If you wish to write a journal entry that celebrates Kwanzaa, think about the seven principles the holiday celebrates. Write about how each principle is present in your life as well as how you would like some of these principles to be more present in your future. Or, write about the ceremonial colors and objects as they appear in your life. Each could offer a particular memory in the form of a vignette.

CHAPTER TEN

Resources to Help Journal Keepers Continue Writing

After a year of journal keeping and using your writing for self-reflection, you might want to continue using the exercises in this book to keep yourself writing, but you might also be seeking sources for additional ideas. You may be curious about other ways keeping a journal can serve you. And you might want to connect with organizations and groups who work with journals and their keepers.

In this chapter, I have included references for more journaling ideas as well as places to get information on journal groups, classes and training in using journal keeping for teaching and therapy. The references will also help you connect with avid journal keepers.

Another way to connect is in groups or online. Many people create or join a writing circle in which the group writes from a particular prompt and then members share what they wrote. In this spirit, in the appendix, I have included a mini-anthology of journal entries by women who each used the exercises in this book.

Books on Journal Keeping

Following are titles of books that you might refer to for further work with your journals. Most are how-to books and/or discussions of writing from life; a few contain excerpts from published journals that serve as inspiring examples.

Adams, Kathleen. *Journal to the Self: Twenty-two Paths to Personal*

Growth. Warner Books, 1990. The author's exercises use dreams, images, unsent letters, lists and stream-of-consciousness writing for healing grief and getting to know one's self.

————. *Mightier Than the Sword: The Journal as a Path to Men's Self-Discovery.* Warner Books, 1994. Dedicated to helping men overcome role models who taught them to constrict their emotions, this book provides, in the author's words, "practical, immediately useful ways to use a journal for personal growth, problem-solving, stress management, creative expression and a whole host of other applications."

————. *The Way of the Journal: A Journal Therapy Workbook for Healing.* Sidran Press, 1998. Adams offers ten-step, quick and easy exercises to help journal keepers write, especially on painful topics.

Aldrich, Anne Hazard. *Notes From Myself: A Guide to Creative Journal Writing.* Carroll and Graf, 1998. The author entries included in this how-to create an enriching approach to keeping a journal.

Albert, Susan Wittig. *Writing From Life: Telling Your Soul's Story.* G.P. Putnam's Sons, 1997. Wittig not only helps the reader write his or her life story, she explains "why we must tell our stories." An invaluable resource for journal writers needing confidence that they are spending their time wisely.

Baldwin, Christina. *Life's Companion: Journal Writing as a Spiritual Quest.* Bantam Books, 1991. This book inspires the use of writing as a tool for spiritual growth. Baldwin believes that, "Everything we learn to write is a stepping-stone for the next level of conversation we are capable of having with ourselves." In writing a spiritual journal, one is expanding the conversation to include one's relationship with the sacred, the beyond or the deep within. Guidance comes from the body, dreams, intuition, sacred ritual, practices of forgiving, love, trust and acceptance. Writing in the journal allows one to access the guidance and develop expertise in the practices.

———. *One to One: Self-Understanding Through Journal Writing.* M. Evans, 1991. "When a person dies, a library is burned." The author heads her introduction with this quote from Edmund White. Journal writing is a way, Baldwin says, of honoring a life, of honoring that writing taps us into our lives and connects us to a "chain of articulation" about being human. Baldwin explores writing to discover inner awareness.

Bender, Sheila, editor. *The Writer's Journal: 40 Contemporary Writers and Their Journals.* Delta, 1997. This anthology features excerpts from the journals of contemporary American poets, playwrights and authors. Writers also contributed essays about how their writer's journals help them create their published work.

Capacchione, Lucia. *The Creative Journal: The Art of Finding Yourself.* Swallow Press, 1988. A guide to discovering and releasing your inner potential through writing and drawing.

Chapman, Joyce M.A. *Journaling for Joy: Writing Your Way to Personal Growth and Freedom.* Newcastle, 1991. A guide for writing on through to the other side!

D'Encarnacao, Paul S., Ph.D., and Pattricia W. D'Encarnacao, M.D. *The Joy of Journaling.* Eagle Wing Books, 1991. The authors provide writing suggestions and remind readers that wisdom found in the Bible and in Eastern thought helps one find true self-development in journaling.

Finlayson, Judith. *Season of Renewal: A Diary for Woman Moving Beyond the Loss of a Love.* Crown, 1993. A blank journal book with pithy quotes as prompts for writing.

Fulwiler, Toby, editor. *The Journal Book.* Boynton/Cook, 1987. This is a collection of articles by teachers who used journal keeping in their classrooms. Their experiences and ideas are helpful to all journal keepers. These teachers found that journal keeping kept students thinking and could be a central mode of learning. The idea of using journals in the classroom is predicated on the learning theorists' findings that "human beings find meaning in the world by exploring it through language—through their own easy talky language, not the language of textbook and teacher."

Gray, Dorothy Randall. *Soul Between the Lines: Freeing Your Creative Spirit Through Writing*. Avon Books, 1998. A book of quirky, enriching thoughts and exercises designed to help you develop emotional insight, character and content.

Heard, Georgia. *Writing Toward Home: Tales and Lessons to Find Your Way*. Heinemann, 1995. After each of her short personal essays of graceful insight and charm, Heard offers writers an exercise from which to write.

Heart, Rosalie Deer, and Alison Strickland. *Harvesting Your Journals: Writing Tools to Enhance Your Growth and Creativity*. Blessingway Books, 1999. Famed author on journaling, Christina Baldwin blurbs this book, "Finally I have something to offer when my students ask me, 'What do I do with all these volumes?'" Here is a whole book of expert exercises to help you find out more about yourself and your life through rereading and considering your journals.

Hinchman, Hannah. *A Trail Through Leaves: The Journal as a Path to Place*. W.W. Norton, 1997. This book by an author and illustrator is a storehouse of ways to use writing and drawing to be more alive in the world.

Holzer, Burghild Nina. *A Walk Between Heaven and Earth: A Personal Journal on Writing and the Creative Process*. Bell Tower, 1994. A fine instrument for helping writers keep and use a journal. Kept in journal form itself, this book demonstrates the creative process and how staying open to the present moment and recording whatever one finds there is important to writing.

Mallon, Thomas. *A Book of One's Own: People and Their Diaries.* Hungry Mind Press, 1995. The author analyzes the significance of diary genres, shares a wealth of information from published diaries and encourages readers to keep their own diaries.

Metzger, Deena. *Writing for Your Life: A Guide and Companion to the Inner Worlds.* HarperSanFrancisco, 1992. Metzger says both the creative and spiritual paths "demand a commitment to truth and a willingness to be trusting, disciplined and aware." Her book is filled with thoughts and examples on how to do this.

Moffat, Mary Jane, and Charlotte Painter, editors. *Revelations— Diaries of Women.* Vintage Books, 1975. A moving and stimulating collection of excerpts from women's personal diaries, including those of Louisa May Alcott, Sophie Tolstoy, George Eliot and Anaïs Nin.

Mosle, Sara. "Writing Down Secrets." *The New Yorker Magazine,* September 18, 1995. A third-grade teacher, working in a predominantly Dominican and African-American community, uses her students' journals to start dialogues with each of them. She realizes the similarities all children share no matter what their background and geography.

Murray, John A. *The Sierra Club Nature Writing Handbook: A Creative Guide.* The Sierra Club, 1995. The first chapter is entitled "The Journal." It discusses those of nature writers and offers ideas for keeping your own. Publication is discussed at the end.

Nelson, G. Lynn. *Writing and Being: Taking Back Our Lives Through the Power of Language.* Luramedia, 1994. In an even, moving and accessible tone, the author provides exercises and examples aimed at using a journal to be present in one's life. His philosophy is well stated: ". . . if I do not say my hurts, do not cry my tears, do not shout my anger, do not tell my stories into the healing skylight of my journal, they will eventually translate themselves into other languages and publish themselves into my very being, into the acts of my life."

Progoff, Ira. *At a Journal Workshop: Writing to Access the Power of the Unconscious and Evoke Creative Ability.* J.P. Tarcher, 1992. These ideas from a master of journaling help you get to know the inner core of your life on ever deeper levels.

Rainer, Tristine. *The New Diary: How to Use a Journal for Self-Guidance and Expanded Creativity.* J.P. Tarcher, 1978. Considered a classic in the field, this book, which famous diarist Anaïs Nin called "revolutionary" and "perceptive," provides techniques for journal keeping aimed at transforming personal problems, discovering joy, overcoming writing blocks and expanding creativity.

————. *Your Life as Story: Discover the New Autobiography and Writing Memoir as Literature.* G.P. Putnam's Sons, 1997. Rainer calls memoir a blend of literature and myth that emphasizes self-discovery. In this book, she offers a history of the genre and discussions about meaning, voice, the dark side, time devices and more.

Rico, Gabriele Lusser. *Pain and Possibility: Writing Your Way Through Personal Crisis.* J.P. Tarcher, 1991. The author states that the very act of putting pencil to paper is an act of giving shape to amorphous feelings. "The act of writing helps name the unnamable: the chaotic feelings we resist, fear or remain unaware of . . . by externalizing feelings in words, we gain a greater ability to take charge of our own lives . . . ." Rico helps her readers explore what she calls the "grammar of the emotions" through astute writing exercises.

Rosenwald, Lawrence. *Emerson and the Art of the Diary.* Oxford University Press, 1988. This critical theoretical study of Emerson's journals contains a thoughtful and instructive chapter, "From Commonplace Book to Journal," valuable for anyone interested in the history of the diary as well as in how Emerson used his.

Sarton, May. Several titles, W.W. Norton. The poet and novelist was also a prolific journal keeper. Following is a list in order of publication:

> *Journal of a Solitude*, 1973
> *The House by the Sea, A Journal*, 1977
> *Recovering: A Journal*, 1981
> *At Seventy: A Journal*, 1984
> *After the Stroke: A Journal*, 1988
> *Endgame: A Journal of the Seventy-ninth Year*, 1992
> *Encore: A Journal of the Eightieth Year*, 1993
> *At Eighty-two: A Journal*, 1996.

Schiwy, Marlene A. *A Voice of Her Own: Women and the Journal-Writing Journey*. Simon & Schuster, 1996. As Jungian therapist Marion Woodman writes in the introduction to this book, "Many women who are finding their own personhood are, at the same time, having dreams in which their teeth are clamped shut by silver braces, or their throats are clogged, or they speak but are not heard." Schiwy's book provides an exploration of how women have been using journals to find their voices and to hear one another speak as well as help for continuing to do this.

Spence, Linda. *Legacy: A Step-by-Step Guide to Writing Personal History*. Ohio University Press, 1997. Linda Spence has created a book that supports and coaches readers in producing personal histories. Her questions and exercises help readers write about "what goes into living a life during your time, in your particular place." The book helps its readers write legacies from their lives.

Story Press, from the editors of. *Idea Catcher: An Inspiring Journal for Writers.* Story Press, 1995. Blank pages with useful writing prompts at the top of each one.

Zinsser, William, editor. *Inventing the Truth: The Art and Craft of Memoir.* Houghton Mifflin, 1987. Authors Russell Baker, Jill Ker Conway, Annie Dillard, Ian Frazier, Henry Louis Gates, Jr., Alfred Kazin, Toni Morrison and Eileen Simpson contribute essays on what editor Zinsser calls "looking for their past with acts of writing."

Centers for Help With Journal Keeping
The Center for Journal Therapy

Founded in 1985 by author and licensed therapist Kathleen Adams, The Center for Journal Therapy's mission is "to make the healing art of journal writing accessible to anyone who desires self-directed change." The Center's vision is "to heal body, psyche and soul through writing." In support of this goal, the Center trains and certifies instructors who teach worldwide. They train and consult with mental health professionals and holistic health professionals and have created a home study program called Clinical Journal Therapy, approved for continuing education credits by the National Board of Certified Counselors. The Center publishes *The Wave* newsletter, which "guarantees you the most up-to-the minute information on workshops, conferences, trainings, intensives and ways to bring instructors to your own community." The Center, now part of the National Association for Poetry Therapy, maintains a Web site where you can find information on journal writing instruction as well as useful references. There are links to groups who offer online writing prompts and support in the use of journaling for attaining specific goals, as well as online subscriber lists that announce news from the center and provide interactive mailings to discuss and share.

The Center's Web site is http://www.journaltherapy.com/wave9 812.htm. Their address is: 12477 W. Cedar Dr., #102, Lakewood, CO 80228. Phone: (888) 421-2298. Fax: (303) 985-3903. E-mail: journaldoc@aol.com.

Center for Autobiographic Studies

Tristine Rainer founded and directs this not-for-profit educational organization "dedicated to promoting the knowledge, appreciation, creation and preservation of contemporary autobiographic works," written for "self-understanding" or "preserving family and cultural history" or for "pooling wisdom."

Her career began with the 1978 publication of *The New Diary: How to Use a Journal for Self-Guidance and Expanded Creativity*. She taught for many years with her famous diarist friend and mentor, Anaïs Nin. The retreats, study groups, newsletter and information from the Center for Autobiographic Studies are valuable for those who journal and may want to concentrate on memoir writing.

The Center for Autobiographic Studies is located at 260 S. Lake Ave., Suite 220, Pasadena, CA 91101. Phone: (818) 754-8663. Web site: http://www.storyhelp.com.

Dialogue House

Dialogue House is a nonprofit organization that houses the late Dr. Ira Progoff's library and sponsors national seminars and classes using his famous intensive journal process published in 1975 as the book *At a Journal Workshop*. The process helps people of different backgrounds, interests and faiths to access creative capacities and gain insights into their personal relationships, their dreams and meaning in their lives. Outreach programs include help for those transitioning from welfare and those in correctional institutions as well as professionals requiring continuing education credits.

Tapes by Dr. Ira Progoff are available. The address is 80 E. Eleventh St., Suite 305, New York, New York 10003. Phone: (212) 673-5880 and (800) 221-5844. Fax: (212) 673-0582. Web site: http://www.intensivejournal.org.

About.com GuideSites (formerly Miningco.com)

At this Web site—http://www.journals.about.com/arts/writepub/journals—Catherine deCuir, a reviewer and contributing editor to many online and print magazines, provides lists of books, tapes, articles and supplies for journal keepers as well as reviews and excerpts from newly published journals. You will find information about classes, conferences, national and international journaling projects and online interactive journal groups as well as articles on journal writing ideas and exercises.

Newsletters and Magazines About Journal Keeping
Story Circle Journal

Story Circle Journal, a newsletter for women with stories to tell, is published quarterly. Written by and for women, this journal aims to encourage its readers to become writers and guide women in setting down their true stories. The sixteen-page issues include how-to ideas on writing chapters of your life, reviews of helpful books, writings by readers, news about the growth of Story Circle Network and notes from Story Circles. A subscription costs twenty dollars a year. Write to: Story Circle Network, P.O. Drawer M, Bertram, TX 78605.

1st Person

1st Person is a quarterly newsletter from Tristine Rainer's Center of Autobiographic Studies. It contains information on autobiography, reviews of memoirs and short personal essays. Available for a twenty-two dollar contribution to the nonprofit center: 260 S. Lake Ave., Suite 220, Pasadena, CA 91101. Phone: (818) 754-8663.

Journal Writer

Journal Writer provides twenty journal suggestions by E-mail for five dollars a month. For samples see their Web site at http://www.w riteplace.com/Journal. Phone: (800) 264-7936. Fax: (541) 686-3562. E-mail: journal@writeplace.com.

❧

There are many more newsletters and zines of interest to journal keepers online. To locate them use the Web site http://journals.abo ut.com/arts/writepub/journals/msub17zine.

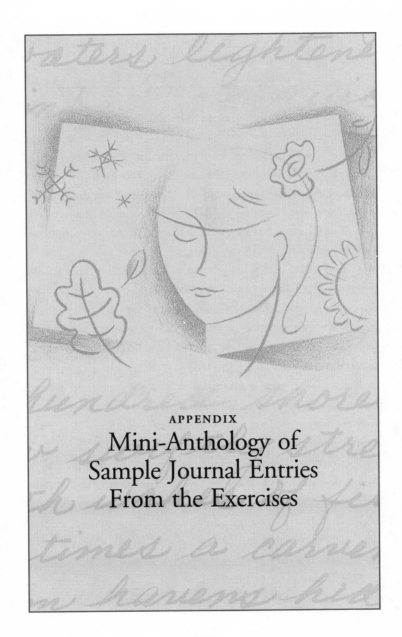

APPENDIX

Mini-Anthology of
Sample Journal Entries
From the Exercises

Reading, Writing and 'Rithmetic,
Taught to the Tune of What I Did

Margaret and the Snipe Hunt

Do teenagers today know about snipe hunts? I rather hope not. They were secretive practical jokes which were neither practical nor funny, especially for the victim. From the distance of almost three quarters of a century, I marvel that I could have been part of such a frightening prank, one in which my best friend was the victim.

Margaret and I lived a few blocks from each other in a northern suburb of Chicago, but we didn't get to know each other until we each became stranded in the fifth grade of what was then known as a "progressive" school, a laboratory for a teachers' college. My parents had pulled me out of the local public school because they were nervous about my early maturing and supposedly unsuitable friendships. Margaret had been in bed for a year with rheumatic fever, and her parents felt she needed a small classroom in a protected environment.

Neither Margaret nor I adjusted to what we considered a weird curriculum and an even weirder bunch of spoiled students and hateful teachers. We survived the year by clinging to each other, and returned happily to our old school the next fall, solid friends for life.

We continued clinging to each other right through high school. Margaret made friends easily, and we soon collected our own tight little clique of about six girls, who gathered in the monstrous, noisy high school lunchroom each school-day noon, sought out "forbidden" movies on the weekend and jealously appraised each other's boyfriends, most of whom were scarcely aware of our existence.

Marcia was an early admission to our self-centered circle. She was an attractive only child whose parents owned a small summer cottage beside a good-sized muddy lake in rural Iowa. Margaret and I were overjoyed when Marcia invited us to share the cottage for a week during summer vacation. I guess her mother thought Margaret and I would be good chaperones when she could not be around.

I don't remember much about that week except that I was proud of my new rubber bathing suit, which was precarious but an improvement over the previous heavy wool suits, and my alarm over the spiders that crawled into my shoes each night and had to be shaken out in the morning. But I do remember all too vividly the snipe hunt.

Marcia had attracted the attention of a local young male, who was probably only a few years older than ourselves, but who seemed marvelously grown-up and sophisticated in his crumpled work clothes which were so unlike the well-pressed shirts and trousers of our high school classmates. Best of all, he had his own wheels, a 1930s version of today's pickup truck.

When he suggested that we go on a snipe hunt, we had to admit our ignorance. He assured us that we would have a good time; it simply involved driving to a large field at night where one person was chosen to hold the bag while the others formed a large circle at some distance and quietly closed in on the center, forcing the snipe into the waiting bag.

I don't remember how or why Margaret was chosen to hold the bag. We left her there in that dark nowhere and then climbed into the truck to begin a slow drive around that wretched lake. I struggled to join in the laughter, but with each bumpy mile my anxiety over Margaret became more acute.

At last we were back in the big, black, empty field. To make up for my unsportsmanlike behavior in the truck, I pretended amused unconcern as we told shivering, frightened Margaret it was all a big joke. Some joke! She scarcely spoke to me for a couple of days. I was too embarrassed to apologize, and we never spoke of it again.

Over the next sixty years Margaret and I never lost track of each other, even though I moved frequently while she continued to live not far from our childhood neighborhood. We saw each other occasionally and always remembered each other's birthday. A year ago her daughter phoned to say that her mother was dying and wanted to talk with me. It was my final chance to say I was sorry about the snipe hunt, but I missed it. Upset, I berated her for not surviving until my birthday. Now I wonder what she would have said if I had apologized at last. To comfort myself, I like to imagine her saying, "You're being silly, Barbara. Snipe hunt? What are you talking about?"

—BARBARA FURNISS

WEEK NINE
Finding the Motto Writer Within

Dear Patient Friend,

Today I am considering going into the bumper sticker business— or rather, I am going into the bumper sticker add-on business. For example, I have long owned a bumper sticker that says, "HELEN KELLER IS ALIVE AND WELL AND DRIVING IN GREEN VALLEY." It hangs on a wall in my garage where it functions as a cautionary admonition each time I back out into the street. When I come to Tucson, I fantasize about having this on my rear bumper with an add-on that shouts, "AND SHE IS DRIVING THIS CAR!" My fantasy, of course, is that this will frighten tailgaters, pickups, California drivers and huge trucks, who will then treat me with extreme courtesy, respect and total avoidance.

—BARBARA FURNISS

WEEK TEN
Metaphor for My Life Right Now

I felt I had to be the strong one. I organized friends and helpers. I organized the building of Catherine's garden. I organized meals, celebrations and gatherings of friends. I organized much of the wedding and the memorial—organizing, doing, doing, doing. I had to be the strong one the morning Catherine died. Allen sobbing in my arms; I was sobbing, too. I had to be the strong one to talk to the hospice nurse. I had to be the strong one when they came for her body. I had to be the strong one that day to get rid of the hospital equipment, and take Catherine's personal belongings and get them out of sight. I was strong helping Allen gather Catherine's favorite objects, her pictures and other symbols of her life to share at the memorial. I was strong to have more than fifty people at the house for food afterwards.

Six weeks later, at a conference center in New Mexico, someone suggested that I would enjoy looking at the labyrinth, something I knew nothing about and had never seen before. The evening light reflected a golden glow off the red cliffs as I walked alone into the hills. There was a warm breeze and the leaves of the cottonwood trees rustled. I came upon a path along which there were stone cairns and feathers tied to branches. The breeze moved a few soft wind chimes. The path led to what looked like interconnecting circles of small stones laid out in the dirt. In the center, there were boulders. Somehow, I couldn't step across the circular stone divisions to reach the center, so, out of curiosity, I began walking from what appeared to be the entrance. I was amazed that as I meandered, I was walking circuitously through all of the circles and slowly winding toward the middle. I kept walking. I was in no hurry. After about twenty minutes I stood in the center. I sat on the boulders and thought about Catherine. I cried and cried. It seemed that the stones held me and I wept for what I had lost and was missing and for the depth of the gift I had given. After some time, I moved out of the circle, retracing the way I had come.

Later, at the conference center library, I found information about labyrinths. I learned that walking the labyrinth has been a meditation tool since the Middle Ages. I learned that the labyrinth is a metaphor for the journey to the center of your deepest self and back into the world with a broadened understanding of who you are. "Yes," I thought, "I went to the center and the boulders held me. I came out stronger for as I wept I became more clear about what I am missing and what I have been given."

—KATHY FRANCIS

WEEK ELEVEN
The Words They Taught Me

Brouhaha
Brouhaha—a laughing witch's brew, cacophonous laughter, seething cauldron, raucous play, tumbling rhymes, confusion, much ado about nothing, whirling dervishes, mayhem, a giant in GULLIVER'S TRAVELS,
fire-breathing dragon, typhoon in Japan, doomsday, baby talk, puff of black smoke, machine-gun stutter, Hare Krishna chant, cold spell, lullaby, Disney Indian princess, bubble bath, champagne toast, Teletubbie, primitive dance, ghost, furry warm blanket, pink haze over the swamp on a sultry day.

—MARA DAVIS

WEEK SEVENTEEN
Confetti: Extension One

Six secrets I am keeping at this time:
1. I practiced law today and I'm not a lawyer.
2. I cringe when my mother calls and I'm busy, but instead of taking the chance of hurting her feelings by immediately telling her I am busy, I chat for a few minutes.

3. I love having my grandchildren over, but get tired fast.
4. I can't tolerate the smell of vinegar.
5. I'm jealous of my ex-husband's girlfriend.
6. I'm insecure about my writing.

Choose one word from each secret:

> Practiced
> Chatted
> Fast
> Vinegar
> Jealous
> Insecure

Word drops out of sky?

PRACTICED: Practiced what? I can't stand secrets. Practiced safe sex? Practiced the alphabet? Practiced tightrope walking? How am I supposed to function if I don't know what this means?

CHATTED: Could be a word from an unknown culture. Depends on how you say it. ch a tt ddd. Could mean "don't jump," could be a formal way of saying "no."

FAST: Means stress—what else could it mean? Don't take your time—do it fast! Means I'm inadequate, I'm not doing it quickly enough. "Jump over that candlestick—fast." Hmmm, maybe it means to hurry for my own good.

VINEGAR: Whew, is that a comment on my breath? An innuendo about my personality? Or a comment about what's really way up there?

JEALOUS: Yuk, don't like this one, feels sticky. Why would anyone drop that word on me?

INSECURE: Looking over each shoulder quickly, she wonders how anyone knew.

—KATHRYN DELONG

WEEK SEVENTEEN
Confetti: Extension Five

The secret: My mother and I both know she is losing her memory but do not discuss it.

The secret is a white feather, small and downy like a feather from the breast of a gull and as snow white and fine as my mother's hair. The shaft is delicate and not strong enough to pull ink from the well. I put it on a scale in the rock quarry where dump trucks filled with stone weigh in before they leave the yard. Of course it registers not at all, and so I move to smaller and more delicate scales knowing they too will not register its presence; it is insubstantial on produce scales, bathroom scales and weight-watchers scales. Only when I put it on a microscale that can sense molecular weight does it register and then mostly the tremor in my own hand. It is so delicate and precious in its perfection, lying there on the scale as if it had worked its way out of the breast of the bird and drifted away unnoticed. I pick it up and hold it in my hand and then paste it into the memory book next to the photographs of my mother as young girl, standing next to the log cabin, hands on her hips, head tilted, eyes glaring defiantly at the man who held the camera.

—JAN HALLIDAY

WEEK SEVENTEEN
Confetti: Extension Five

The Secret and How Much It Weighs:
Thought it was going to be heavy but I could carry it. Put it on the kitchen scale and it hardly registered. How can that be when it feels so heavy? It's irritating that this thing affects me so hard but doesn't really exist. It could blow away or evaporate if it weren't for the weight in my chest anchoring the damned thing. If I could only

send it off to where it should go, I'd weigh less. Hmmmm, a new way to diet—by telling secrets!

—KATHRYN DELONG

WEEK TWENTY-FIVE
Burying the Dutch Oven

Today I am going to bury you. You are so beautiful: pink and white, shiny (like a rippled seashell), heart-shaped with the hands of mother and infant reaching out to touch amongst floating flowers.

Yet I am so terribly sad to give you up. You who are the only tangible reminder of my dearest friend. A true love gift. But, I know where our journey will end. It will end on the beaches of Florida's Siesta Key. A beach that he and I walked so many times— holding hands, seduced by the waves and the sun.

I will dig a medium-sized hole in the sand, right near the edge of the sea. There the sand will be moist enough for me to carve out a tiny crater to accommodate you. I will take a small child's shovel and chip steadfastly away at the sand packed tight by repeated footsteps. It won't take long because you are so small.

I will dig a hole by the sea. A hole to consecrate the place where we took our walks, on so many sunlit days, six years ago. God knows—I do not want to bury you. You who sit on the counter in my living room and shed an iridescent glow upon my life. A glow of seashells, sand dollars, whispered dreams and memories of what could have been.

But bury you I must, in order that my life might go on. To bury you is to bury the part of him that lives in my home weeping unshed tears into the stillness of my heart. To bury you is to wipe away the sadness and the pain of yesterday and embrace the joy of today.

And yet I will insist upon a tiny fence around the mound and marker just inside of it. The way that sea-turtle eggs are protected from trampling feet at hatching time. The marker will say, with all due simplicity, " Given and buried with love. Please do not disturb."

—MARA DAVIS

WEEK TWENTY-EIGHT
Each Side a Balance

My Two-and-a-Half-Pound Dumbbells

I love you because you have padded grips that I can squeeze tightly and feel powerful.

I do not love your hot pink ends that contain a removable weight, screwed in, jiggling as my triceps quiver.

I love you because you are heavier than my old blue two-pound weights. You feel more substantial than those, more where I am now.

I do not love you because you are not three-pound dumbbells like the ones bodybuilder Joyce Vedral uses on the cover of the *12 Minute Total Body Workout* that I'm using to feel and to grow all my body's muscles.

I remember Barbie at the Afton Village swimming pool in Houston, Texas. Barbie was a lifeguard. It was probably 1966 or 1967, and she wore a bikini—brightly colored, possibly even the fuchsia of my weights. Barbie's mother was dead, her father supported her and her younger brothers and she took care of those boys all the time. She'd flirt, she was popular, she had a power. She was athletic and female.

And so it is with my hot pink two-and-a-half-pound dumbbells.

—CHRISTI KILLIEN

WEEK TWENTY-EIGHT
Each Side a Balance

Hair dryer

I love you because you blow consistent hot wind in just the right strength, a shaft of wind that flattens out that curl that has always flipped up on the right side, the same curl, that in the eighth grade ruined the perfect symmetry from a night of sleeping on the bristles of soup can-sized brush rollers. My hair was wound especially tight on that wayward right side, but it was a foggy Northwest morning and I had to stand outside in the damp air for the school bus. By the time my turn came to pose for the photographer that curl had flipped up. Thirty-five years later I am still trying to tame it. The left side is quite docile, surrendering itself to the heat and lying down in an orderly manner, but that right side is strong willed and will do what it damn well pleases. You are the only hair dryer that can work with it. I don't love you because I am quite sure that you will someday short out on me while I stand naked in the puddle of water on the floor. They'll find me there on the floor, with you clenched in my right hand, my hair dried naturally all in waves and sticking out every which way. And the troubling thing is that when one is electrocuted, there's a freezing that occurs as the shock travels through your body—when it hits there's no time to clutch the towel on the way down—so you'll be found sprawled out there, all naked and blue, all indiscreet fat revealed for the paramedics, who in this town are people I know. And one of the reasons I don't like you is that sometimes, in what seems to be pure capriciousness on your part, you suddenly stop and I mistake the silence for a bolt of electricity surging into my body. I leap into the air and fling you across the room—and tethered to the electrical plug you slam back into my legs, then lie there dangling at the end of your cord. I wonder how much I am losing in years from the surges of adrenaline coursing through my body when this happens. I love you because although I've flung you many times you never break when I fling you. I also love you because your little filter plugs up with dust and the only way to unplug it without hurting you is to sit down and pick the lint out of each little hole with a toothpick. Of course you are unplugged when I do this. There's something satisfying in having the time to get you all cleaned up—it must be similar to the feeling chimps have as they pick the lice out of each other's hair. I do hate your noise though, interrupting the morning quiet, signaling in such a rude way that the day begins. When I use you, I know I am headed out the door rather than sitting at my desk for hours. It's a mixed feeling, however. Sometimes I am inspired in my morning shower to write something and wrap up in my towel and go directly to my desk, not pausing for vanity, and write until I am through—sometimes until 2 P.M.—still in the towel and with hair that has dried every which way. But when I use you first thing—well with hair this beautiful, and a little lipstick on, mascara, a bit of blush on both cheeks, a spray of perfume—I'm out the door.

—JAN HALLIDAY

WEEK THIRTY
Private Moments: Extension Two

Temptation

Each Sunday evening, Dad, Mom and I climbed into our 1942 green Plymouth sedan with the silver three-masted sailing ship hood ornament and rode the half hour to Aunt Vena and Uncle Frank's house in Elmhurst. Vena and Frank were my mother's aunt and uncle, the same ages of my grandparents. Their house reflected the graciousness of their times: doilies placed on the arms and backs of chairs and the sofa, lace dresser scarves falling from mahogany lamp tables. On the coffee table was a cut glass candy dish filled each week with a different delectable candy. Sunday was the one evening that Mom and Dad would go out to a movie, leaving me to sit on Uncle Frank's lap by the big floor-model console radio and listen to Charlie McCarthy. Aunt Vena would offer me a piece of candy, cautioning me not to take one until we checked with my parents upon their return to see if I could have another.

Charlie McCarthy always said funny things that a five-year-old and an old uncle laughed at, and it was safe and secure to laugh with someone who loved you and had his strong arms surround you. After the radio program was over we would play games like Hangman and Connect the Dots at the coffee table next to the overflowing cut-glass candy dish. My hand would, on its own, find its way to rest an inch or two away. Aunt Vena, knitting, often concentrated on her knit and pearls and Uncle Frank often looked away from our game to converse with Vena. But if I snuck a candy would they still adore me? I couldn't risk it, but I wonder.

—JUDY TOUGH

WEEK THIRTY
Private Moments: Extension Three

If I'd snuck back yet another time into the yard I'd planned and planted, I could have birds nesting here in the birdhouse now. I would fill that verdigris Victorian bird feeder every time before it got empty. I bet Ed's new wife forgets to fill it. I bet the vibes are so bad there that no birds will occupy that birdhouse. With all the action at the birdhouse and the feeder, my hunter cat would have a greater variety of prey.

Oh hell, the truth is I'd forget to fill the feeder for days at a time, just as I do with the cheaper replacement a friend gave me. Lori probably fills that feeder before it's one-third empty. She cooks meat and potatoes every night. I'm sure she feeds the birds, too.

The truth is I didn't take the birdhouse and bird feeder because they would have known who did it. Who else would want them enough to steal them? Who else knows the defeat of being physically barred from your own house and possessions on the last day of moving yourself and your kids out? Who else would care that I'd bought one at Eddie Bauer and ordered the other from a catalog in my attempts to make that house feel homelike. It never did. It always felt cold to me. When I go to the door now to pick up the kids on Sunday nights, the house smells like meat and potatoes. I open the car window because the meat smell clings to the kids' hair and clothes. I'm mostly vegetarian, though as consistent with that as with feeding birds.

I didn't take the birdhouse and bird feeder because to take them would be to get down off my high horse. I wanted to stay above such things. Or to be perceived to be above them. Or to not get caught.

I don't think they ever realized the last time I snuck back into the house. Breaking and entering, it could have been called, though I didn't break anything—the door was unlocked. I'd run into Lori at the mall, swimsuit shopping with four kids, two of them mine. That would take her awhile. I took only things they wouldn't notice—two bathroom rugs, a towel, my special lanolin-coated dustmop (also from a catalog), one more place setting of silverware. Homely items from my tenure of housekeeping.

—JULIA ROUSE

WEEK THIRTY
Private Moments: Extension Four

My black coat, the wool one with the asymmetrical flap across the chest, the one with a Renoir button on the lapel, was in my sister's car. She was borrowing it and had loads of other clothes in the car for consignment. She came back from a play to find her car broken into and the clothes all draped out over the concrete embankment of the parking lot. I imagine this as if the thief was shopping, laying things out, and the only thing taken, the only thing was my coat. And I imagine the thief examining all of the clothes—which to take? Did he or she try them on? And my coat was chosen. I knew when Leslie told me the story why the coat was taken. Because it was a cool coat; it made you look good. It wasn't too heavy, but you could scrunch it up under your neck—that asymmetrical flap—and it was flattering, that dark wool.

And then I bought my current coat and knew it had the same magic. It's a black velvet swing coat with a hood and large gold button at the throat. Its design and fabric work magically together, and I do not leave it or loan it out. Except once. It was perfect as part of my daughter Annie's Halloween witch's costume.

—CHRISTI KILLIEN

WEEK THIRTY-TWO
Gratitude

Thank you, Herman, for berating me for putting vines on the back of my house. Thank you, also, for forcing me to uproot and move the small orange tree that I planted on our mutual turf.

Thank you, because you forced me to be less selfish, less territorial, and to honor your eighty-six years, thirty of them lived in our mobile home park. You forced me, in your stubbornness, to honor your age and your humanity, and to take a look at my own arrogance in infringing on your longtime domain. You showed me that I could move from anger to compassion and that we could transcend the limitations of "I" and "mine" by moving into a realm of brotherhood.

We nodded, at first, while gardening. Polite nods, softening the icy stares above the hedges. Then, one time, you said: "Hello, Mara." And I said: "Hello, Herman." From time to time we would make small talk: "How are you feeling Herman? How's Mary?"

"Nice day. Oh, we're doin' okay, I guess. My back hurts a lot since I had that fall. Mary can't see well anymore. But we're doin' fine. Thanks for asking."

From casual banter, it progressed to concern. "Is your back doing better?" I would ask. "Do you need anything today?"

My son went away to a drug treatment center. You noticed his absence and asked where Josh was. I surprised myself by telling you, because you cared enough to ask about him. I didn't tell the other neighbors where he was.

We went beyond the anger, Herman. We went beyond the icy stares, beyond my pulling your weeds when you were too sick to pull them yourself, beyond the roses and the hibiscus, and my tears when they carried you out on a gurney. We moved from fear to love and understanding. We did it quietly, with very few words, the two of us.

I thank you for that: giving me the gift of love and understanding. You taught me that at eighty-six. I'm sorry that I never got to say good-bye. I will miss you, my friend.

—MARA DAVIS

WEEK THIRTY-SIX
Admonitions

I don't remember many admonitions when I was growing up as the youngest of five children. We never locked our door or experienced crime, and I loved to be alone in the house in that Southern California neighborhood.

The admonitions I recall were from my years in Catholic school beginning with: "Don't play with non-Catholics; they have no chance to go to heaven. This could affect your chances at eternal life." Most of the admonitions were spoken as commands: Walk in a straight line. Keep your desk clean. Bring money for the poor. Tuck your shirt in. Write in blue ink.

Now that I think of it, the Ten Commandments were little more than admonitions:

Don't steal, Don't kill, etc.

Those made sense to me. They still do.

But other admonitions were nothing but invitations to my devious friends and me:

Don't loiter on the way home from school.

Don't go behind the stage curtains.

Don't go near the convent.

Don't go on the stage.

Don't climb the fence.

Don't climb the school yard trees.

Don't enter the building at lunchtime.

Don't trade food.

Don't talk in church.

My absolute favorite was, "Don't laugh in church."

That only made everything about church all the more interesting and potentially funny:

Priest as father. The fancy silk embroidered vestments in every color of the rainbow. I used to wonder how much those were worth.

Altar boys we knew to be bad boys but who looked so angelic in their vestments. The church itself, stone cold and somber, filled with young, vital and energetic kids herded inside to be serious by anxious and angry nuns.

Not that anything funny ever actually happened in church. It really wasn't a funny place. But the potential was there, and that was enough to fuel our fire and made us giggle, snort and howl at nothing. This behavior led to the predictable admonition that I wrote by the thousands and keep in a box to this day:

I will not laugh in church.

I will not laugh in church.

I will not laugh in church, etc.

—SUZANNE WILLSEY

Admonitions

It's the middle of the morning, and Lucille and I have been talking on the telephone. She is one hundred years old, still living by herself in the apartment that she has occupied for thirty-five years. I want to talk about the many admonitions that are thrown at elders. You know them: get some exercise, keep busy, don't do so much, get some rest, keep warm, take your medications, let us know how you are feeling, don't complain.

The list goes on, as long as a child's. The rebels counter with their own advice on old age. Writer Alice Walker recommends wearing purple. Dylan Thomas admonishes "Do not go gentle into that good night." My friend Lucille has had time to evolve her own charming, manipulative way of dealing with age and sees no need to talk about something as unpleasant as admonitions. She launches into what is on her mind.

She has received an invitation to a citywide party for people ninety-nine and older, and she has not decided how to respond. The word she gets is that there was dancing at last year's party, and that worries her a bit because she relies on a small cane to steady her tiny, elegant body. She also is troubled by the questionnaire which asks for the number of grandchildren and great-grandchildren. She has a nice passel of these, but is dubious about sitting around swapping numbers with other centenarians.

"Besides," she declares, "My grandson Ralph is fifty years old. Why would I want to talk about him?"

I try unsuccessfully to bring her back to the subject of admonitions while the conversation veers in several directions, mostly about the handsome, intelligent men like my husband who have not been to see her lately. We are in the process of saying good-bye when this indestructible woman, who is old enough to be my mother, recalls her winning bridge game the day before and concludes firmly, "Barbara, you should play bridge." Thus admonished, I send her love and put down the phone.

—BARBARA FURNISS

WEEK THIRTY-SIX
Admonitions

I know there are so many admonitions I have heard throughout my childhood, but the one that rings loud and clear was told to me by my mother when I was around sixteen and it has stayed with me ever since: "Never go out of the house without lipstick on." I really wasn't sure how that would affect my everyday life, but I have always stood at attention when a pronouncement came from my mother. After all, wasn't she the harbinger of the right things to do? When I first heard it, I would think to myself, "My God, what would happen to me if I didn't listen?" Would I be arrested for having colorless lips? Would people start talking about me as the person who doesn't wear lipstick? Tsk, tsk. For many years, I always made sure my lipstick was applied evenly and correctly and that I blotted it just the right number of times. The epitome of this admonition came when my mother was experiencing chest pains while staying at my house. It was 5:00 A.M. and she came into my room saying that I had to take her to the emergency room. Of course, I quickly threw on a T-shirt and some sweats and drove to the hospital as quickly as I could. She was admitted promptly and given morphine to ease the pain. The drug put her into a somewhat sleepy stage and it was during one of these morphine-induced states that she awoke, looked up at me and said as only a mother could, "Marlee, why don't you put on some lipstick?" Need I say more. I wonder if that's why I can never find a lipstick I like. They are always too red, too orange, too brown, too pink or just plain ugly. There are many times that I do leave the house without lipstick and I have to say that I feel a little undressed when I do. The admonishment has left a lasting effect, although I can't say that any lipstick has done the same. There's a moral to this story somewhere.

—MARLEE MILLMAN

WEEK FORTY-ONE
Self-Portrait, Self-Portrait on the Wall

Portrait of Mrs. Keep-Everybody-Happy

This self-portrait had to be done in erasable colored pencils, because over the years it required a lot of upkeep and adjustments so that it would look good wherever it was hung. Full-time happiness creation requires effort; revisions are frequent, control must be maintained, denial kept in readiness. If the lines are kept just right the portrait might make a good commercial—the toothy smile in place, everything just so. But for what? The perfect suburban home and family? The best toothpaste or laxative?

It was hard on the family, of course, because truthfulness has no place in this portrait. No talking back, no making trouble, above all NO unhappiness. No matter how hard the artist works, the tired eyes are never quite right. Occasionally they even show a hint of panic. Finally the portrait had to be thrown out. As life continued, the erasures destroyed it. Good riddance I think.

—BARBARA FURNISS

WEEK FORTY-FOUR
Hide-and-Seek

I had several sets of cousins and each home had their favorite game. At the Laniers', Red Rover reined across their huge front grassy yard and at Vertress', Flagman hailed in the street, but at Griggs', their pick was always Sardines. They lived three miles outside of a small community, down a graveled road, past a cemetery on a sweeping curve and finally at the top of an emerald hill. The yard roamed gracefully down on all four sides and disappeared into the neighboring woods and fields.

The house was limestone, painted a pale soft green with large white trim windows and doors. The rooms were large and inviting with shiny wood floors dotted with patterned area rugs. One evening in January we decided to play the game Sardines and since the weather outside was a frigid twenty-three degrees, we voted to try it indoors. We closed off the back end of the house and the boundaries included three bedrooms with deep stuffed closets and a long, narrow blue bathroom. The lights snapped off, leaving all seven of us in pitch-blackness. The sudden darkness invaded our space and it seemed my hearing was swallowed up and gone.

My older brother was the chosen surveyor of a hiding place and off he crept in his white sock feet. On the count of ten the remaining six of us began our groping around the edges of bedposts, trunks and chairs and carefully tried to recall which direction the Victorian lamp stood. After some time of bumping into each other, stubbing a toe and bouncing your forehead off of a pointed dresser corner, I was the fourth one to find the secret hiding place. I plunged my hand through the hanging fringe from a chenille bedspread and grabbed an elbow. I slid under with as little noise as possible, trying to contain my glee. I was now safe. I laid on my back, facing a set of exposed bed springs that I could not see, hoping my long blonde hair would not get tangled between the coils.

So far, we had four under one twin bed and shortly thereafter, the other two joined us. Every possible effort was made not to giggle while pushing a foot out of your ear, or butt away from someone's face, or thumb up a horrid place such as a nose. Randy was the youngest and last one out. He had already lost, but intuition whispered to all of us to drag this out as long as possible. At that time Randy was seven and still did not talk clearly. Actually he had developed his own jargon and become quite comfortable with it and only the immediate family could decipher what he said. His sock feet sauntered into the room, hesitating to enter. He stood at the threshold; no doubt his little heart hammering against the stillness and cave-like surroundings. No noise, dead silence, we were all holding our breath, the sweat popping across our foreheads like tiny silver BBs.

Eventually a tot's voice spoke over the dead, "Whare eh couboui?" (Where is everybody?) No one dared to move. Again, with a bit more volume, "Whare eh couboui?" Monty's hand was stuffed over his mouth and the snort pilfered around his curled fingers and drove the rest of us to shreds of giggles. Randy raced to the bed, pulling the bedspread up and peered underneath with relief, "Oh caroh qu arh!" (Oh there you are!) We all hooted and hollered twice as much rolling and clawing our way from under the twin bed.

Now in his early forties, Randy is still considered the baby. When we all get together, those of us that are left, this one tiny scene is shared over and over and never has lost its special humor of when we were all so very young and having so much fun. I for one would be daring enough today to play Sardines with all my wonderful cousins.

—SALLY SHOWALTER

WEEK FORTY-FIVE
Whistling

The Guitar

I learned how to play the guitar in my senior year of high school. I was seventeen years old. I remember that my teacher, Henrietta Frieberg, was a middle-aged, heavyset woman, with reddish brown, disheveled hair. I also remember that at a time in my life when I was confused, lonely and yearning to break out and discover who I was, she was an ally in a world of mostly hostile adults. She was my anchor. Her apartment, to me, was a sunny oasis.

Henrietta was not like other adults. They were conventional and boring. She was offbeat and freewheeling. Our souls were one. I loved folk music and she was able to teach me how to play and sing the songs that I loved. I was shy and self-conscious around people, but never around Henrietta. She disciplined, encouraged and appreciated me. She was, in her capacity as teacher, the parent I didn't have at home.

I remember her saying to me that in playing the guitar I would be more than just a pretty young girl, because I would also be able to play an instrument. The year was 1960. In those years women were ill-defined creatures who traded a lot on their looks and femininity. My parents were convinced that all a girl needed to get ahead were her looks, breeding and perhaps an education at a worthy institution. Then she could catch a wealthy husband and live happily ever after. Henrietta implied that there just might be more involved in becoming a woman. I always thought so. Now I found out that Henrietta thought so too.

I played guitar all through my senior year of high school. I played when I was happy, sad and even when I was despairing of life. I played when I had a boyfriend and I played when I was alone. And I found out that I could also sing. And every week, I continued my lessons with Henrietta.

I left Henrietta when I went off to college in 1961. I don't remember ever seeing her again. But when I went away my faithful Goya went with me. I entertained at dinners and at fraternity parties. No one laughed, and secretly I always felt so proud to be more than just a pretty face.

I kept that guitar close to me for years, long after I had ceased to play. It had developed a small crack. When my children were young I put it high up on a bookcase so that they would not destroy it. But eventually they knocked it off the shelf and it shattered beyond repair. Reluctantly, I threw it away.

The guitar meant nothing to my children but it meant everything to me. It stood for years of growing up and breaking out of a mold and finding out who I wanted to be. It was passed to me in friendship by the only adult that I considered a soul mate. It transported me from teenager to adult, from girl to woman. It showed me that I was so much more than just a pretty face. I was a creative human being.

I don't know exactly why I started to play the guitar, except that there were things inside of me that needed to be expressed. And I don't know exactly why I stopped playing either. Even now, years later, there are times when I think about the joy of playing the guitar and the hours spent with Henrietta. There are times when I wish that I had the comfort of the strings again. And I say to myself: "Maybe tomorrow I will buy another Goya and take lessons ." And who knows. Maybe tomorrow I will.

—MARA DAVIS

WEEK FORTY-SIX
Starvation Hill: Extension One

Freedom is a black-and-white photo of the dancer Baryshnikov standing on his right leg, muscles tensed, right arm extended outward, left leg extended waist high in back of him, while his left arm is raised and slightly curved above his head. His head is turned to the left, tilted slightly downward, eyes closed and mouth open.

There is no indication of where he came from or where he may be going. He is simply a being suspended in time. A soul in flight. He relaxes into the moment. His mind is at peace with his body.

It seems as if his body is performing a superhuman feat, balanced so precariously in space, while his face reflects enormous tranquillity. He makes the impossible seem effortless. Baryshnikov. A magician-sorcerer casting spells conjured up in netherworlds. He defies gravity, time and age by refusing to move on. There is nothing as sacred, complete or stubborn, except the innocence of childhood.

I remember this feeling of perfect freedom from when I was a child of about ten. I was walking home from school with a group of girlfriends on a sunny spring day. It felt glorious to be alive and young. All at once we all started to skip and sing in our youthful exuberance. We sang a song that I believe was from Peter Pan that was popular at that time.

The words to the song were as follows: "I won't grow up, I don't wanna go to school, just to learn to read and write, and recite a silly rule." We kept on skipping and singing these words louder and louder, with utter determination.

With all of the innocence of childhood, I really believed that in singing these words with my friends, we were somehow willing time to stand still, in a stubborn refusal to grow up and grow old. It was both a declaration and a prayer cast out into the universe.

Like Baryshnikov we defied gravity, time and age by refusing to move on. And just like this famous dancer we took total control of one glorious moment. For an instant we seemed to have wings. For just one instant, we made the impossible feel effortless inside our young souls. There can be no greater feeling of freedom than this.

—MARA DAVIS

EXERCISE FORTY-SEVEN
Getting Here

My Dad always made us leave in the middle of the night. Or at least it seemed like it.

"There's nothing in Kansas worth seeing so you won't miss a thing," growled Dad as he and mother shuffled my brother and I into our 1959 jet-black Delta 88 Oldsmobile. Mom rushed around to the rear of the car, ordering Dad how to put the odds and ends of plaid and stripped luggage in the oversized trunk. I was eight and Terry thirteen. This trip to Denver was my first that I can remember and we made several more over the years to come. Sometimes we took cousins, aunts, uncles and even Grandma.

The big Oldsmobile with its sleek tail fins swam up and down the hills and valleys through Missouri and on into the night, crossing the state line into Kansas. My parents always occupied the wide front seat, the soft yellow glow from the dashboard lights illuminating quiet profiles. Periodically the interior light snapped on and Dad moved the map a little closer, squinting at the crooked red and blue lines on the map that read "Courtesy of Phillips 66 Gasoline."

My brother stretched out over the entire back seat while I fluffed two pillows, one on each side of the hump on the floorboard. One of my grandmothers had given me a stuffed rabbit, soft, cuddly and yellow with a white belly and pink nose. His name was Mopsy. He, too, slept on the floor, the pavement beneath our ears whizzing by only a few inches below us. The following year, Flopsy would join us on our trips to Denver, she being pale blue, white round tummy and long floppy ears. Those two rabbits went everywhere. One of the last trips at age fourteen, I couldn't bear to leave the two behind tucked in my bed with all the other dolls and animals. My folks thought I was too old to take the extra baggage; therefore, I smuggled them inside the pillowcase that I used to sleep on. We had a glorious time.

On the car droned through the night and dawn approached through the back glass, creeping lazily, resting on our sleepy faces. We had not yet passed all the way through Kansas. Dad was right, there was nothing. The road grew longer and longer with each passing incline. Terry and I rested our chins on the back of the front seat, eyes wearing out for something to look at. No trees, no bushes, just one long strip of highway running forever into the future. Every now and then my brother would let out a very long sigh. Mom fiddled in her purse, passing out chewing gum or hard butterscotch candy. I wondered if my whole summer would be spent driving down this road to nowhere.

By lunch we were well into Colorado, although the scenery wasn't much fancier. Eventually by midafternoon the Rockies jumped up so quickly they seemed like a painting held up at an auction. Snow in June? Unbelievable. But there it was, white as could be, the entire horizon swelled with the Rocky Mountains. We grinned and gawked, "Can't you drive faster? Let Mom drive, she'll drive a lot faster." And she would, too. The speedometer was a long rectangle that took up half the dashboard. The reading turned colors as the mph increased, white up to 40, then green to 80, then red to 120. Mom liked staying in the red hot zone until Dad leaned over with his upper lip drooping over his lower one, and with a disgruntled frown at being caught, she dropped it back to the cool green zone.

Not only did Mother bear a lead foot, she also had the best sniffer any of the family had ever experienced. Dad said she surely was a hound dog in another life. At one point in the trip, my brother had slipped out the dreaded deadly silent gas and Mom quipped, "All right, who got into the potato chips? That is a potato chip stink," and she was right, Terry had eaten the potato chips.

The tall pines soon began popping up like mushrooms in the spring, the sky turning bluer and bluer, and the air so crisp and dry your words crackled like ice in a glass. We arrived at our great-uncle Roy's home up in the mountains. Their eleven-year-old son,

Stephen, bounded off the porch in three leaps, running toward our car shouting, "They're here, they're here!" We all climbed out of the car, stretching, chattering with Uncle Roy and Aunt Edna and all trailed into their tiny, but neat home with Flopsy and Mopsy tucked under each of my arms.

—SALLY SHOWALTER

Mara Davis currently resides part of the year in Tucson, Arizona, and part of the year in Sarasota, Florida. She obtained her M.S.W. from New York University in 1972 and practiced as a therapist in New York City. After retiring from the field, she became a competitive ballroom dancer and writer. She has had one poem published.

Kathryn DeLong is a graduate gemologist who works as a jewelry appraiser and makes jewelry in her home studio. She edits *The Northwest Newsletter* for the Northwest Federation of Mineralogical Societies, facets colored gemstones and has a precious stone import business.

Kathy Francis lives in Seattle and Port Townsend, Washington. She recently retired from paid work as a teacher, social worker and health administrator. Since retirement she has become an art student at a Seattle community college and an art institute. Kathy says, "I love following a long-held desire to paint as well as having more time for family and friends. I hadn't realized how precious time is; now that I am retired, I am much more aware of how I use it."

Barbara Furniss is currently being released from the restrictions of a 1940s overdose of academic degrees. At the age of seventy-seven she is finding out that writing really is fun.

Amy Jo Greene writes she is "a domestic goddess ruling over my roost of three teenage daughters and a remarkable husband in Tucson, Arizona. I was raised here after my parents divorced, leaving the life of the Air Force brat to live the life of a sun worshipper. I graduated from college only to return home to marry Prince Charming."

Janice Goodman is a lifelong Chicagoan who spends winters in Tucson. She is working on a reminiscence of her life growing up in the late 1940s and 1950s which she hopes her children will enjoy enough to pass along to her future grandchildren. She has a head full of ideas and is wishing for the time (and talent) to complete the task.

Jan Halliday has lived in and out of Port Townsend for twenty years. At first she went to the beach every day and arranged rocks in a straight line according to color. She felt guilty about this, so she had a baby, helped remodel fourteen houses, wrote three travel guides and about one thousand magazine and newspaper articles. Having reached the age of menopause, she is seriously considering a return to the beach.

Marjorie Hilts is a former New York actress now performing with Blood Hut in Tucson, Arizona. She writes her own material.

Christi Killien and her husband and three children live in Suquamish, Washington. She works at the Northwest Adoption Exchange in Seattle, writing bios that appear in a photolisting book and on the Internet for foster children awaiting adoption. Christi co-wrote, with Sheila Bender, *Writing in a New Convertible With the Top Down: A Unique Guide for Writers*; she's published six novels for children, numerous essays in literary magazines, and is at work on an adult novel.

Marlee Millman moved to Tucson four years ago from Chicago.

With the desert and mountains as her inspiration, she hopes to make writing a priority in her life.

Julia Rouse has used journal writing for many years to develop emotional honesty, creativity and her spiritual life. She was cofounder and editor of *Life Scribes: A Collective Journal,* a newsletter for journal and diary writers. A psychotherapist in private practice, she lives with her partner and two children in Port Townsend, Washington.

Sally Showalter has lived in Arizona for the past twenty-four years. Her passions are gardening, experimental cooking, painting and writing, mainly fiction. She shares her time with her husband, grown children, four cats and a dog.

Judy Tough continues to write after early success in her retirement with poetry and essays. Recently, she has been a counselor to children through a nonprofit center in Port Townsend, and she has learned to weave.

Suzanne Willsey has taught English and elementary school internationally for the past sixteen years. She has recently returned to her desert roots to teach in Tucson for now. Journaling is a part of her routine wherever she is.

A

Abraham, Pearl, 119
Absence and Presence (Neruda), 153
Accordion Crimes (Proulx), 58
Adams, Kathleen, 182
Admonitions, 119-121, 202-206
Affirmations, 84-85
After Death: How People Around the World Map the Journey After Life (Miller), 156
After the Stroke: A Journal (Sarton), 181
Albert, Susan Wittig, 176
Albom, Mitch, 52
Aldrich, Anne Hazard, 5, 176
All I Really Need to Know I Learned in Kindergarten (Fulghum), 135
Allen, Steve, 10, 13
Angela's Ashes (McCourt), 123-124, 147
Angelou, Maya, 131
Anticipation, 148-150
Art of Fiction, The: Notes on Craft for Young Writers (Gardner), 9
At a Journal Workshop: Writing to Access the Power of the Unconscious and Evoke the Creative Ability (Progoff), 180, 183
At Eighty-two: A Journal (Sarton), 181
At Seventy: A Journal (Sarton), 181
"Azaleas" (Meinke), 127

B

Baldwin, Christina, 2, 15, 176-177
Bantock, Nick, 110

Before and after, 89-90
Beginnings, 160
Bender, Sheila, 177, 216
Blake, William, 5
Body parts, 133-135
Book of One's Own: People and Their Diaries, A (Mallon), 179
Bottom Line/Personal magazine, 10, 13
Bridges of Madison County, The (Waller), 131
Brown, Helen Gurley, 12-13
Buzbee, Lewis, 144

C

Campbell, Joseph, 151
Cantwell, Aileen, 161
Capacchione, Lucia, 177
Care of the Soul (Moore), 133
Carlson, Dr. Richard, 112
Carter Clay (Evans), 137
Casewit, Curtis W., 2
Castaneda, Omar S., 2
Center for Autobiographic Studies, 183-184
Center for Journal Therapy, 182
Chapman, Joyce M.A., 177
Childhood games, 135-137, 206-208
Childhood memories, 114-116, 123-124, 170-171
Childhood trips, 140-142, 211-214
Cliches, 49, 144
Clustering, 16-19
Clustering exercises, 16-19, 57, 61-65, 87-88, 90-91, 98-99, 113, 123-124, 128, 134, 143, 146
Commitment issues, 30-33

Cosmopolitan magazine, 12-13
Creative Journal, The: The Art of Finding Yourself, 177
Creativity, journaling and, 10-13
"Crossing Brooklyn Ferry" (Whitman), 82

𝒟

Davis, Mara, 20, 28, 192, 196, 202, 210-211, 215
De Mille, Agnes, 3
"Dear Journal-to-Be" exercise, 17, 19-22, 28
Death, 156-157
deCuir, Catherine, 184
DeLong, Kathryn, 193, 195, 215
D'Encarnacao, Patricia W. and Paul S., 8, 177
Descriptions, 82-83, 92-96, 130-140, 142-144, 210-211
Dialogue House, 183-184
Dialogues to overcome critical voices, 48-52
Diary, The: A Complete Guide to Journal Writing (Casewit), 2
Dillard, Annie, 28
Divakaruni, Chitra Banerjee, 67
Don't Sweat the Small Stuff . . . and It's All Small Stuff (Carlson), 112

ℰ

Eating, 116-117, 144
Emerson and the Art of the Diary (Rosenwald), 180-181
Emerson, Ralph Waldo, 29
Endgame: A Journal of the Seventy-ninth Year (Sarton), 181
Endings, 158-160
Epigraphs, 27-28
Evans, Elizabeth, 137

ℱ

Family Circle magazine, 88
Finding seeds method, 83-84
Finlayson, Judith, 177
1st Person, 184
"Five-and-Ten, The" (Shore), 114
"Food and Happiness" (Simic), 142
Francis, Kathy, 192, 215
Frazier, Ian, 87
Freewriting, 43-44
Fugitive Pieces (Michaels), 118
Fulghum, Robert, 135
Fulwiler, Toby, 177
Furniss, Barbara, 21, 39, 190, 205-206, 215

𝒢

Gardner, John, 9
Gelb, Michael J., 11
Getting Here (Weiner), 140
Ginsberg, Allen, 107
Glenn, Helen Trubek, 158
Gnostic Gospels, 10
Golden Mean, The (Bantock), 110
Good Housekeeping magazine, 88
Goodman, Janice, 38, 216
Graham, Jorie, 22
Gratitude, 112-114, 201-202
Gray, Dorothy Randall, 27, 83, 178
Greater Phoenix Area Writing Project, 11
Greene, Amy Jo, 23, 215
Griffin and Sabine (Bantock), 110

ℋ

Halliday, Jan, 194, 198, 216
Hartley, William G., 2
Harvesting Your Journals: Writing Tools to Enhance Your Growth

and Creativity (Heart and
  Strickland), 178
Hass, Robert, 107
Heard, Georgia, 178
Heart, Rosalie Deer, 178
Hellenga, Robert, 2
Hemley, Robin, 2
Henry Fool, 126
Here Lies My Heart anthology, 144,
  155
Hillman, Brenda, 10
Hilts, Marjorie, 216
Hinchman, Hannah, 178
Holidays, 160-174
Holzer, Burghild Nina, 178
House by the Sea, A Journal, The
  (Sarton), 181
How I Learned to Drive (Vogel),
  127-128
*How to Think Like Leonardo da
  Vinci: Seven Steps to Genius Every
  Day* (Gelb), 11
Huddle, David, 167
Hugo, Richard, 104

I

"I Name You Queen" (Neruda), 23
I Never Told Anybody (Koch), 60
*Idea Catcher: An Inspiring Journal for
  Writers* (Story Press), 181-182
*If I Had My Life to Live Over I Would
  Pick More Daisies* (Martz), 109
Inner critic, 50
Insight, 4-6
Intensive Journal Workshop, 7
Interruptions, 64-66
*Inventing the Truth: The Art and
  Craft of Memoir* (Frazier), 81, 87,
  182

J

Jesus Christ, 10, 165-166
Job description, 37-41, 150
Johnson, Tim, 90
Journal
  naming, 22-24
  physical attributes, 16, 25
  sample entries, 187-213
Journal Book, The (Fulwiler), 177
*Journal to the Self: Twenty-two Paths
  to Personal Growth* (Adams),
  175-176
Journal of a Solitude (Sarton), 181
Journal Writer, 185
*Journaling for Joy: Writing Your Way
  to Personal Growth and Freedom*
  (Chapman), 177
Joy of Journaling, The (D'Encarnacao
  & D'Encarnacao), 8, 177

K

Karenga, Dr. Maulana, 173
Kathleen, Adams, 175-176
Kazin, Alfred, 81-82
Keen, Sam, 156-157
Kennedy, John F., 71
Killien, Austin, 28
Killien, Christi, 196, 201, 216
King, Dr. Martin Luther, Jr., 163
Kirchner, Bharti, 154
Koch, Kenneth, 60

L

Lamott, Anne, 139
Landers, Ann, 56
Leaves of Grass (Whitman), 81, 105-
  106
*Legacy: A Step-by-Step Guide to
  Writing Personal History*
  (Spence), 181

Lessons, 57, 127-130
Letter to columnist, 56-57
Letter of introduction, 39-41
Letters to a Young Poet (Rilke), 53-54
Levertov, Denise, 2
Life occasions, 153-160
Life Scribes: A Collective Journal, 217
Life's Companion: Journal Writing as a Spiritual Quest (Baldwin), 2, 176

M

Mad money, 25-27
Making Sense of Suffering (Stettbacher), 8
Mallon, Thomas, 1, 179
Marry Your Muse: Making a Lasting Commitment to Your Creativity (Phillips), 64
Martz, Sandra Haldeman, 109
Matthews, William, 10
Mayes, Frances, 116-117
McCourt, Frank, 123-124, 147
Meinke, Peter, 127
Metaphors, 71-73, 125-126, 190-192
Metzger, Deena, 179
Michaels, Anne, 118
Midsummer Night's Dream, A (Shakespeare), 164
Mightier Than the Sword: The Journal as a Path to Men's Self-Discovery (Adams), 176
Miller, Alice, 8
Miller, Sukie, 156
Millman, Marlee, 24, 206, 216-217
Mirroring exercise, 122-123
Moffat, Mary Jane, 179
Moore, Thomas, 133
Morris, William, 155

Mosle, Sara, 179
Mother Journeys: Feminists Write About Mothering (Nemiroff), 166
Motto writing, 69-71, 190
Mroczek, Dr. Daniel, 9
Murray, John A., 179
"My First Trip to Florida" (Weiner), 140
Myss, Caroline, 15

N

Naming your journal, 22-24
National Association for Poetry Therapy, 182
"Negative Space" (Glenn), 158
Nelson, G. Lynn, 11, 103, 179
Nemiroff, Greta Hoffmann, 166
Neruda, Pablo, 23, 153
New Diary, The: How to Use a Journal for Self-Guidance and Expanded Creativity (Rainer), 180, 183
New Yorker Magazine, The, 179
Nin, Anaïs, 179, 180, 183
Notes From Myself: A Guide to Creative Journal Writing (Aldrich), 5, 176
Nye, Naomi Shihab, 67

O

Objects
  mundane, 105-108, 196
  as symbols, 111-112
"Ode: Intimations of Immortality from Recollections of Early Childhood" (Wordsworth), 157
Oliver, Mary, 35
One to One: Self-Understanding

Through Journal Writing
(Baldwin), 15, 177
*Opening Up: The Healing Power of
Confiding in Others*
(Pennebaker), 8
Opposites, 110-112

P

*Pain and Possibility: Writing Your
Way Through Personal Crisis*
(Rico), 180
Painter, Charlotte, 179
Parade Magazine, 56
Pearsall, Paul, 9
Pennebaker, James W., 8
People Magazine, 96
Perry, Daneen, 27
Phillips, Jan, 64
Place
  observation, 53-56, 74-76
  owning unfamiliar, 104-105
Poetry Handbook, A (Oliver), 35
Polon, Linda, 161
Preconceived ideas, 100-101
Privacy issues, 29-30
Private moments, 109-110, 198-102
Progoff, Ira, 7, 180, 183
Proulx, Annie, 58

R

Rainer, Tristine, 180, 183, 184
Reader's Digest magazine, 96
Recipes, 108-109
Recovering: A Journal (Sarton), 181
Resources, 175-185
Revelations—Diaries of Women
  (Moffat and Painter), 179
Rico, Gabriele Lusser, 180
Rilke, Rainer Maria, 12-13, 53-54

Romance Reader, The, (Abraham),
119
*Roots of Evil, The: The Origins of
Genocide and Other Group
Violence* (Staub), 13
Rosenwald, Lawrence, 180
Rouse, Julia, 200, 217

S

Sabine's Notebook (Bantock), 110
Sarton, May, 181
Saving oneself, 118-119
Sayings of others, 121-123
Scenes, making, 145-158
Schiwy, Marlene A., 7, 15, 181
Schwartz, Morrie, 53, 74
*Season of Renewal: A Diary for
Woman Moving Beyond the Loss
of a Love* (Finlayson), 177
Seasons, 61-64
Secrets, 85-87, 127-130, 192-195
Self-consciousness, 47
Self-discovery, 4
Self-portrait, 130-131, 206
Self-reflection, 76-79, 99-101, 124-
126, 150-152
Seventeen magazine, 89
Shakespeare, William, 164
Shameful experience, 58-61,
188-190
Shea, Lisa, 10
Shiva Dancing (Kirchner), 154
Shore, Jane, 114
Showalter, Sally, 208, 214, 217
*Sierra Club Nature Writing
Handbook, The: A Creative Guide*
(Murray), 179
Simic, Charles, 142
Similes, 55
Snyder, Gary, 96

"Songs to Survive the Summer" (Hass), 107
Soul, 5-6, 133-135
Soul Between the Lines: Freeing Your Creative Spirit Through Writing (Gray), 27, 83, 178
Speaking up, 145-158
Spence, Linda, 181
Spiritual Quests: The Art and Craft of Religious Writing, 100
Springsteen, Bruce, 103
Star Book, 96
"Starvation Hill" (Warn), 138
Staub, Ervin, 13
Stettbacher, J. Konrad, 8
Stevens, Wallace, 36
Story Circle Journal, 184
Story Press, 181-182
Strickland, Alison, 178
"Supermarket in California, A" (Ginsberg), 107

T

Taylor, Elizabeth, 147
Telephone, 144-145
"The ____ of ____" exercise, 131-133
"Things to Do While ____" exercise, 96-98
"Thinking About My Father" (Huddle), 167
"This is My Last Affair" (Buzbee), 144
Thomas, Dylan, 204
Thoreau, Henry David, 29, 47, 62-63
Thoughts
  preconceived, 100-101
  trying on new, 66-67
Time management, 35-36

"To See a World in a Grain of Sand" (Blake), 5
Tough, Judy, 199, 217
Tourist within, 67-69
Trail Through Leaves, A: The Journal as a Path to Place (Hinchman), 178
Transcendentalists, 29
Traveling Mercies: Some Thoughts on Faith (Lamott), 139
Triggering Town, The (Hugo), 104
Troubleshooting, 43-45
Tuesdays With Morrie: An Old Man, a Young Man and the Last Great Lesson (Albom), 52-55
23 Charring Cross Road, 126

U

Under the Tuscan Sun: At Home in Italy (Mayes), 116-117
"Unemployed Fortune-Teller, The" (Simic), 142

V

Visions and Voices series, 36
Voice of Her Own: Women and the Journal-Writing Journey, A (Schiwy), 7, 15, 181
Vogel, Paula, 127
Vogue magazine, 89
Voice, 14, 48
Voice-over, documentary, 54, 75

W

Walk Between Heaven and Earth: A Personal Journal on Writing and the Creative Process, A (Holzer), 178
Walker, Alice, 204
Walker in the City, A (Kazin), 81

Waller, Robert James, 131

Warn, Emily, 138

Wave, The, newsletter, 182

*Way of the Journal, The: A Journal
Therapy Workbook for Healing*
(Adams), 176

*Webster's II New Riverside University
Dictionary,* 30

Weiner, Fred, 140

Whistling, 137-138, 208-210

Whitman, Walt, 81-82, 105, 107

Whole Earth Holiday Book, The
(Polon and Cantwell), 161, 163

Williams, William Carlos, 36

Willsey, Suzanne, 38, 203, 217

Window observations, 53-56, 74-76

Woman's Day magazine, 88

Woodman, Marion, 5, 7, 181

Words people taught you, 73-74,
192

Wordsworth, William, 28, 157

*Wouldn't Take Nothing for My
Journey Now* (Angelou), 131

*Write Your Own Pleasure
Prescription: 60 Ways to Create
Balance and Joy in Your Life*
(Pearsall), 9

*Writer's Journal, The: 40
Contemporary Writers and Their
Journals,* 2, 10, 67, 177

Writer's journal, defining, 1-7. *See
also* Journal

*Writer's Rules, The: The Power of
Positive Prose—How to Create It
and Get It Published* (Brown), 13

*Writing and Being: Taking Back Our
Lives Through the Power of
Language* (Nelson), 11, 103,
179-180

Writing categories, 78

*Writing in a New Convertible With
the Top Down: A Unique Guide
for Writers* (Killien and Bender),
216

"Writing Down Secrets" (Mosle),
179

*Writing From Life: Telling Your
Soul's Story* (Albert), 176

*Writing Toward Home: Tales and
Lessons to Find Your Way*
(Heard), 178

*Writing for Your Life: A Guide and
Companion to the Inner Worlds*
(Metzger), 179

Y

*Your Life as Story: Discover the New
Autobiography and Writing
Memoir as Literature* (Rainer),
180

Z

Zinsser, William, 100, 182